A PROTESTANT CASE
FOR LITURGICAL RENEWAL

A
PROTESTANT
CASE for
LITURGICAL
RENEWAL

by
Kenneth G. Phifer

PHILADELPHIA
THE WESTMINSTER PRESS

264
P543P
1965

LIBRARY OF CONGRESS CATALOG CARD No. 65–13493

Acknowledgment is made for the use of quotations from William D. Maxwell, *An Outline of Christian Worship: Its Development and Forms;* London: Oxford University Press, 1936; Ray C. Petry, editor, *A History of Christianity: Readings in the History of the Early and Medieval Church;* © 1962, by Prentice-Hall, Inc.; Hans Lietzmann, *The Founding of the Church Universal;* Charles Scribner's Sons, 1938; and for those appearing on pages 17, 19, 23, 67, 84, 106–107, from Ilion T. Jones, *A Historical Approach to Evangelical Worship;* copyright 1954, by Pierce and Washabaugh (Abingdon Press).

PUBLISHED BY THE WESTMINSTER PRESS ®

PHILADELPHIA, PENNSYLVANIA

PRINTED IN THE UNITED STATES OF AMERICA

To my wife
whose sensitivity to that which is
meaningful in worship has always
encouraged me

Contents

Preface

This book has grown out of a long-felt need on the part of its author, a need that roots in a parish ministry of seventeen years. When I graduated from seminary and went to Franklin, Tennessee, to assume responsibility for conducting worship services, along with the other duties of a pastorate, I found I had no resources except a hymnbook and some vague ideas based on what study I had done in the psychology of religion. My denomination had a *Book of Church Order* which I had purchased while in seminary and which contained a " Directory for Worship." I quickly found that its archaic directions were so general as to be meaningless. In 1946 the Presbyterian denominations published a revised *Book of Common Worship*. So little was heard of it in the South that my first copy was purchased in 1952. In the meanwhile I had experimented, improvised, and simply worked out orders of worship that seemed to combine some aesthetic values with such pragmatic considerations as when people should stand and for how long at a time. My shelves contained two good books on worship, *Ascent to Zion*, by Samuel Arthur Devan, published by The Macmillan Company in 1942, and *The Public Worship of God: A Source Book*, by Henry Sloane Coffin, published by The Westminster Press in 1946. They helped to orient me, but neither professed to be more than an introduction and neither afforded guidance in ordering the worship of the local congregation except in a very general way.

Since those days, many books on worship have been published, drawing on history, psychology, and ecumenical practice. Seminaries have introduced required courses on Christian worship. The average minister is more aware of its importance than he has been since the Reformation. No longer does he consider everything " preliminary " to the sermon. I have written for the purpose of drawing together some of the historical background that gives a context to contemporary worship in such a way that the minister will have a perspective on the liturgical trends in the mid-twentieth century. It is my hope that the intelligent layman may find some help in understanding why it is and how it is that the life of the church still comes to focus in corporate worship. Changes in worship practices are not easy. The minister who hopes to introduce his people to the great resources of the church must know them. Some congregations will respond eagerly; others will manifest massive inertia or active hostility. In many places changes must come about gradually. Less friction may develop and more intelligible participation be encouraged by a congregational committee who will spend time in evaluating denominational heritages and ecumenical resources. It may be that such a committee would find this book useful. I have not attempted to disguise my conviction that the present interest in renewal, through worship, of the life of the church is a mark of real vitality and hope.

No given order of worship is suggested, for several reasons. Most denominations now provide their clergy with some type of service book containing suggested orders in line with their tradition. The 1960 General Conference of The Methodist Church authorized *The Book of Worship* containing proposed revisions for trial use through 1964. Although not bound to the Sunday service of John Wesley, the order of worship is based on that adaptation of the Church of England service. The Congregationalists have a service book that provides its clergy with liturgies and forms representative of the whole church. In keeping with their heritage of freedom, the services are suggestive and optional. The Joint Committee on Worship of the Presbyterian Church in the United States and The United Presbyterian Church in the United States of America has provided the ministers of those denominations with a *Service for the Lord's Day and Lectionary for the Christian Year* which, after a period of trial, will, with whatever modifications seem necessary, form the core for a further revision of *The Book of Common Worship.* The interesting feature of all these service books and of their suggested orders of worship is the basic similarity they display as they explore the traditional and attempt to wed it to the contemporary. Many congregations will reject the order suggested by their denomination as too ritualistic. The local minister and his worship committee are the only ones who can evaluate how far they can go in reestablishing the features of corporate, Christian worship which have been so mutilated by a gradual process over a period of centuries.

In addition to the denominational resources, consideration may be given to such a service as that provided by the Church of South India, which may be found in T. S. Garrett's *Worship in the Church of South India* (John Knox Press, 1959), or in *The Book of Common Order* of the United Church of Canada. Each of these is a service produced in an ecumenical atmosphere and intended to minister to congregations drawn from varied traditions.

Because personal experience enters so largely into the background and purpose of my writing, I cannot indicate adequately the contributions that have been made by the congregations I have served in the First Presbyterian Church of Franklin, Tennessee, the Oakland Avenue Church of Rock Hill, South Carolina, and the Presbyterian Meeting House of Alexandria, Virginia. They were patient congregations who never protested experimentation and entered with me into pilgrimages toward new places of worship. Dr. L. C. Rudolph, my colleague and professor of church history at Louisville Presbyterian Seminary, examined the original draft painstakingly and made invaluable suggestions. Dr. Roland Bainton, in spite of being hospitalized because of a painful accident, graciously put me on the trail of material that helped clarify for me the part played by Huldreich Zwingli in the development of Protestant worship. Dr. Arthur Hall, of the Central Presbyterian Church of Louisville, Kentucky, gave me the reactions of a parish minister who has done much to lead his congregation into deeper worship experiences. Mrs. Raymond Carter, director of Christian education for the Joint Synods of Kentucky, afforded helpful insights and gave me encouragement to feel that such a thesis as mine would be an aid to ministers and laymen who sometimes are uncertain of the meaning of the current " liturgical renewal." Mrs. Katherine Wilson typed the original manuscript and Mrs. Keith Kensinger prepared the final drafts. To them as well as to my wife and daughter, who accepted the laborious task of proofreading, I am grateful. In the background there are other unnamed people to whom I am grateful for love and inspiration and without whom this book would not have been written. Of course I alone am responsible for its contents.

People like my parents — to use their own matchless phrase — attended places of worship. Now that I see that old phrase with a fresh eye, I also see how astonishing it is. Places of worship. How much we have lost, we of the younger generation, by having no places of worship! Perhaps this new world must remain desolate at heart until it achieves new places of worship. Then the spirit of Man will come home again to the Universe. — *J. B. Priestley* [1]

CHAPTER 1

Introduction

Some years ago in a planning session for a national youth convention one young man suggested: "Let's make the worship services brief and snappy. We've got a lot of work to do." This cavalier treatment of worship is not uncommon among Protestants, unfortunately. This attitude of getting the act of worship over with so that we can get on with the business of the Kingdom is often unconscious and quite sincere, but is no less deplorable for all its unconscious nature and naïve sincerity. As a matter of fact, it is even more deplorable because it is unconscious and because there is no deliberate blasphemy in it. It reflects the casual attitude that Protestantism is a faith of sermons and service, resolutions and revolutions, propaganda and projects. It gives the impression that although there is a time for tipping one's hat to God, the demands of life are so pressing that a vital religion must keep that time to a minimum so that the true believer may be up and about more tangible and important business. Herbert Wallace Schneider [1] makes the point that it is typical of the American sentimental and individualistic tradition that this stanza of Coleridge's poem should be very familiar:

> "He prayeth best, who loveth best
> All things both great and small;
> For the dear God who loveth us,
> He made and loveth all."

whereas the following stanza has a foreign sound:

> " O sweeter than the marriage-feast,
> 'Tis sweeter far to me,
> To walk together to the kirk
> With a goodly company! "

Enough has been said about American activism. However, the emphasis frequently has been to set contemplative theology over against activism as a corrective. Perhaps the truest perspective is gained as we set forth worship as the framework within which both theological thought and acts of service are to be carried out. There is a very real sense in which worship precedes both thought and act, for worship alone appeals to the total personality. It is only through worship that the entire man is reached. When Paul Tillich affirms that the problem of our age roots in the fact that we have no symbols to point beyond the age, he is describing a problem in worship. We relate through worship to that which is beyond, not through intellectual contemplation. We feel the Presence as we engage in worship wherein we respond with our whole beings to the Mystery. This is why worship is as old as man. " Man is a worshiping animal," says Baudelaire. Plutarch wrote long ago: " If you go through the world, you may find cities without walls, without letters, without rulers, without houses, without money, without theatres and games; but there has never yet been seen, nor shall be seen by man, a single city without temples and gods."

It must be said, however, that although the impulse [2] to worship remains universal, there is confusion as to the meaning and nature of worship as an act. Within the context of American society, especially Protestant American society, this confusion is encased in a bland formlessness. Many of us are given to bromidic vagueness: " To work is to pray," we say with unction. We give vent to nonsense about nature as the setting in which we worship best. Actually, an increasingly urban society is so far removed from a real feeling of personal dependence upon nature that at best nature worship is sentimental and artificial. A rugged mountain peak, a vast canyon, a colorful sunset, or a gigantic waterfall may strike us with temporary awe and may call forth an overwhelming aesthetic reaction, but our withdrawal from direct relationship to mountains, canyons, weather phenomena, soil, and water prevents us from seeing these expressions of creation as vital symbols pointing beyond themselves and drawing us into a meaningful experience of God. I can remember feeling a lump in my throat and a mist in my eyes while driving through the Tetons in Wyoming. I turned to my wife and found her actually crying in the presence of such sheer beauty. In essence, however, the experience was aesthetic, and we brought to it an already formulated faith in a Creator God. In an age when men were more intimately connected with the earth, nature's manifestations could speak in symbolic fashion in a way in which they seldom speak today to the average American Protestant.

Meanwhile, more direct symbols are lacking in vigor. "An honest description of Protestant worship must begin with a judgment upon it," writes Robert McAfee Brown. "Few things seem more chaotic. . . . Many ministers conduct worship without any apparent sense of mystery and awe and wonder in the face of what they are doing." [3] The feeling of indifference in regard to the discipline of public worship is notorious among Protestants. Perhaps less complaining on the part of the clergy and less exhortation to church attendance as a duty is in order. The time and energy might be better spent in an evaluation of what has happened to Protestant worship. We might well take more seriously the fact that our failure in this area of church life is a failure to understand the nature and importance of worship. Furthermore, our failure in this respect may well be the heart of our failure to relate vitally and totally to our culture. Few men in the twentieth century have been as aware of the social implications of the gospel as was William Temple, late Archbishop of Canterbury. He was vigorous and outspoken in the causes of economic justice and peace. No one could possibly accuse him of evasion of the ethical implications of the Christian faith or of any attempt to flee the hard-nosed realities of ordinary living through advocacy of " pie in the sky bye and bye." Nonetheless, it was Archbishop Temple who made what he himself confessed " many people will feel to be a quite outrageous statement " in a little book published in the midst of World War II: " This world can be saved from political chaos and collapse by one thing only, and that is worship." [4]

If worship is the hope of the world, we might well be conscientiously examining its place in the life of the church. Much confusion reigns among Protestants because of a vague sense that our practices are not as meaningful as they might be, combined with a hazy desire to do something, compounded by a helpless feeling as to what to do. In consequence we decorate our services with bits of lacy fringes. We set the choir to marching in processional, encourage them to sing fluffy " Amens " as " responses " to prayers, fill out the silence in the service with " organ interludes." We give a call to " silent " prayer during which the organist plays " Sweet Hour of Prayer." We spot a few symbols here and there about the sanctuary, push the Communion Table back against the wall, and swap our white socks for black socks in the pulpit. We have gone " liturgical " and are more than pleased when someone who formerly said, " I enjoyed the sermon," now says, " It was a sweet service." It still does not jell, however, and somehow we know it. We add a few more choir " responses," put additional candles on the altar, and have done with it.

On the other hand, there are many stubborn souls who will have nothing to do with the liturgical movement. They see in it a return to Rome and a dark betrayal of the Reformation. They insist upon the old ways and even assert that

the new interest in the rituals of worship indicates an effort
to escape the ethical and theological involvements of Biblical faith. They fear that preaching will be denigrated. They
see in symbols a danger to vital evangelical worship. Ilion T.
Jones affirms a " common agreement among scholars that,
generally speaking, the degree to which people employ
symbols in worship depends upon the degree of their intellectual development. The most extensive use of symbols is
found among ignorant and primitive peoples. The more lit-
erate people become and the more facilities they develop
for communicating through words, the less they either desire or require symbols in worship." [5] The difficulty with
such a sweeping generalization based upon " common
agreement among scholars," none of whom are cited, is that
it is impossible to worship without symbols just as it is impossible to communicate at all without symbols. Language
itself is symbolic. It began with gestures and vocal utterances that were purely emotional and were associated with
particular occasions such as terror or overwhelming joy.[6]
As time went on, the voiced utterances came to represent
associated emotions and with the further passing of time,
man evolved particular sounds to convey specific meanings. Language was born, and through the symbolism of
language men were able to communicate more directly with
each other than is possible through signs and gestures.
Words are a more immediate form of symbolism of ideas
but they remain symbols.

In religion, language falls back upon other symbols to
express realities that are otherwise inexpressible. Donald
Baillie points to the vast number of spatial metaphors in our
language about spiritual realities. " When we say: ' The
Lord is in His holy temple,' or ' Lift up your hearts. We
lift them up unto the Lord,' or ' Come down, O Love divine,' or ' Feed me with food divine,' we are using spatial
and material metaphors, ' up ' and ' down ' and ' come '
and ' feed.' And how can we avoid it, if we are to say anything at all? " [7] How are we to represent the spiritual di-

mensions of reality at all, unless we represent them by way of symbols? We simply face a choice of symbols. Protestantism has, since the post-Reformation period, relied largely upon verbal symbols — creeds, formulations of confessions of faith, preaching. The faith of Protestantism has been passed on from generation to generation by means of its expression in words. The verbal symbols of the faith were not isolated appeals to intellectual apprehension. They appealed to the whole man. They spoke in a vivid way to generations of men whose understanding of reality was structured within the framework of the age of reason. The symbols of Protestantism, resting primarily upon verbal communication, were most natural to the world of the seventeenth, eighteenth, and nineteenth centuries in Western Europe and America. The use of logical deduction, abstract concepts, and propositional theology spoke to men in terms that conveyed meaning. Now it is questionable whether such symbolization is as effective. No longer can we believe that our deductions, our concepts, our propositions, our verbalizations, correspond with exactness to reality. Our understanding of truth is always proximate at best. Our language represents our understanding. It does not contain truth. Therefore, to purport to speak to the intellect with the assumption that once the intellect is reached, communication is established with the whole man is to fall into the pitfall of rationalism.

It is certainly true that Christianity is dependent upon creeds, confessions of faith, and preaching, and that Protestantism, especially, has made its impact upon the world through the dominance of its verbal symbols whereby understanding of the revelation of God in Jesus Christ our Lord has been communicated. It is certainly not true that these verbal symbols can be replaced or pushed aside. Preaching is still the essence of Protestant power. We need not less preaching but more and better preaching. At the same time we need to enrich our services with a broader use of other than verbal symbols. We must not lose the didactic element that Dr. Jones insists "must predominate in evangelical worship if it is to be preserved in its true form." [8] However, we must reexamine what is didactic in the twentieth century. "Didactic" is that which is "fitted or intended to teach." What is fitted to teach the modern mind? Do men learn only, or even primarily, through direct teaching in verbal form, through explanation and exposition? The structured reasoning of our Calvinistic forebears, the authoritative declarations of propositional nature that were once effectively didactic, would seem to be so no longer. They do not edify. Modern preaching at its best reflects this change. It is no longer characterized by the "didactic" approach of the nineteenth century. It is an existential, life-centered stressing of relationship. Worship, as the framework for preaching, must partake of the same approach. The fact that this is sensed by so many ministers in nonliturgical churches has led to the experimentation and change that we see going on around us. Alexander Miller delineated the true form of the church under four aspects: Worship, Doctrine, Discipline, and Outreach. Of worship he says: "Much of our Protestant worship is simply not edifying. It has neither true Catholicity nor true Contemporaneity. It is shapeless, superficial, sentimental, subjective." [9] If such an indictment is true, what can we do about it? Where should we begin?

To edify, worship needs to be truly catholic and authentically contemporary. It must have shape and depth, valid emotional appeal, and vital objectivity. Where are the resources for such qualities? First of all, we may need to ask ourselves what worship really is. Interestingly enough, few nonliturgical leaders have ever sought to define it. Luther once referred to the word "worship" as meaning "to stoop and bow down the body with external gestures; to serve in the work." [10] Calvin, Knox, and the other Reformers would seem to have thought of worship solely in terms of the rightness or wrongness of various practices. They evidently made no attempt to analyze or define. Such endeavors were to come much later. The " psychology of worship " is modern both as a term and as a field for study and research. In liturgical churches the concept of worship has been structured around the Eucharist. Although the word " liturgy " may now be defined as " pertaining to public prayer or worship," its ordinary usage in Christian terminology has been in reference to the form used in cele- bration of the Mass. Its broadened usage in contemporary studies of worship is perfectly valid, but its more restricted meaning is indicative of the approach of such groups as the Orthodox, the Roman Catholic, and the Anglican.

The approach to be made in the chapters following will therefore be based primarily upon the historical and tradi- tional practices of the church universal. Out of an examina- tion of these practices should come insight into what is truly catholic. Only then will consideration be given to the authentically contemporary with due regard to the tre- mendous contributions of those who have brought the in- sights of psychology to bear upon worship from the stand- point of human needs and response. The question as to what worship is at this point therefore focuses on a study of those worship practices which have been characteristic of the Christian church from its inception to modern times.

CHAPTER 2

Temple, Synagogue, and Upper Room

To understand Christian worship it is necessary, first of all, to examine its roots in Judaism. The two major centers of worship for the Jew at the beginning of the Christian era were the Temple and the synagogue. In terms of direct influence, there is no doubt of the supremacy of the synagogue. In terms of the worship ideal, there is no doubt of the all-pervading influence of the Temple. It was to the Temple that the devout Jew looked for his supreme experiences in worship. It was here that he felt that the awesome Presence of his God was uniquely manifest. It is important that we remember this fact in the beginning, for there is the tendency to assume that the only influence of importance on the worship practices of the early Christians was the synagogue with its informality, its high degree of lay participation, and its large element of didacticism. In the background there was always the Temple with its scrupulous ritualism, its priesthood, and its Mystery. Even though the average Jew made but few pilgrimages to the Temple during an entire lifetime, he was aware of its rites and dedicated to its perpetuation as the focus of his religious community. Each day at the Temple the office of burnt offering was performed both morning and evening. As part of this central service fixed prayers were offered by priests and by people. The incense offering was a high moment of praise. The service of music was central to the offering of praise and thanksgiving. The first Christians, therefore, were accustomed to a special priesthood, to a liturgical order of service with congregational participation, to a ritual of prayer, to music and song, and to a sacrificial system.

Alongside of the influence of the Temple, and unquestionably more directly important, was the practice of the synagogues of Judaism. The synagogue system apparently had its inception in the period of the Babylonian exile when, separated by distance from Jerusalem and the Temple, the people of Israel gathered together in less formal worship experiences. The didactic element was foremost as the emphasis was placed on the law. Priestly functions were not observed and the interpreter of the law attained prominence. The teacher was the central figure in the synagogue. Lay participation came naturally. Upon the return to Palestine, the importance of the synagogue in Jewish life increased rather than diminished. Estimates as to the number of synagogues in Jerusalem at the beginning of the Christian era are impossible to make with any degree of accuracy. They were numerous. At the time of the fall of Jerusalem in A.D. 70 there were approximately four hundred. It was in the synagogue that the Christian movement gained impetus and it was from the synagogue that many practices passed over into Christian worship with very little change.

As outlined by Gamaliel II, synagogue worship involved two main divisions, the liturgical and the instructional. The services incorporated the use of psalms, the recitation of the Shema, the offering of the eighteen Benedictions, readings from the Law and usually from the Prophets. In addition, opportunity was often given the reader to comment on the lesson from the Law or the Prophets (Luke 4:16-29). The basic elements of Christian worship are quite evident here. Adaptation was made, changes were introduced, and modifications came about as the Christians, caught up in a living faith, sought the most meaningful expressions possible for that faith. But essentially, Christian worship was rooted in synagogue worship and was a de-

velopment of it within a Christian framework. Ilion T.
Jones affirms that it " became the cradle of the Christian
church and the forebear of Protestantism." [1]

We may put together, then, the Temple and the synagogue as joint progenitors of Christian worship, with due
recognition that the synagogue influence was predominant
and far more direct. As Christianity moved out from Jerusalem among the Jews of the Dispersion and among the
Gentiles, the Temple as a creative factor was even less significant. That it was not wholly dissipated can be affirmed,
for the New Testament retains many traces of the sacrificial system as the developing theology of the Lord's Supper testifies.

However, we must not view early Christian worship as a
combination of Jewish practices with an admixture of Gen-
tile adaptations. Christian worship became something new
and different. C. F. D. Moule is right to insist that " Christian worship, like Christian literature, was continuous with,
and yet in marked contrast to, Jewish worship. . . . Christian worship was continuous with Jewish worship and yet,
even from the first, distinctive." [2] This distinctiveness was
manifested in the materials used in worship. From the beginning the Christians used the writings of their own
leaders such as Paul and verbal recollections of incidents
from the life of Jesus and sayings attributed to him. With
the passing of time, the writings attained equal authority
with the Law and the Prophets. The pericopes concerning
Jesus were combined into larger bodies of material and before the end of the first century the Synoptic Gospels had
been assembled. From earliest times the Christians used the
psalms as their spiritual forebears and compatriots of the
synagogue used them. In addition they composed Christian
hymns, some fragments of which are to be found embedded
in the New Testament. It is assumed that Eph. 5:14,
" Awake thou that sleepest, and arise from the dead, and
Christ shall give thee light," along with I Tim. 3:16, " God
was manifest in the flesh, justified in the Spirit, seen of an-

gels, preached unto the Gentiles, believed on in the world, received up into glory," are such fragments. Paul's famous passage in Phil. 2:5-11 on the self-emptying of Christ would seem to be either an early hymn or a confession of faith. The book of Revelation has many examples of primitive Christian hymnody, and the canticles of Luke, chs. 1 and 2 — the Magnificat, the Benedictus, and the Nunc Dimittis — are products of the ecstatic and fervent outbursts of musical praise natural to a people nurtured on the books of psalms.

The Christian leaders encouraged such compositions. In the letter to the Ephesians, Paul writes, " Be filled with the Spirit, speaking to yourselves in psalms and hymns and spiritual songs, singing and making melody in your heart to the Lord " (Eph. 5:18-19). The Colossians are exhorted: " Let the word of Christ dwell in you richly in all wisdom; teaching and admonishing one another in psalms and hymns and spiritual songs, singing with grace in your hearts to the Lord " (Col. 3:16). This willingness on the part of the early church to introduce new material into the basic synagogue structure of their worship marked their gatherings as distinctive from those of their Judaistic neighbors.

The major contrast with Jewish worship, however, came at the point of the Lord's Supper. The origins of this distinctive rite are obscure, but its primitive nature is plain. In some way from the very beginning the followers of Jesus associated a special meaning to the breaking of bread together in his name. Furthermore, a particular meal that he shared with his disciples shortly before his death came to be a symbolic experience through which Christians were to share the significance of that death. The narratives of the Synoptic Gospels identifying this last supper with the Passover vary in their accounts of the words of Jesus. The outline of what Dom Gregory Dix calls " The Shape of the Liturgy " remains the same. Bread is broken and given to the disciples with the words: " This is my body." A cup is passed with an invitation to drink of the " blood of the covenant which is poured out." John, who directly contradicts the Synoptics in their identification of the last meal with Passover, contains no parallel to the special nature of the Last Supper with the disciples as the Synoptics present it. Instead, he moves the whole " This is my body " concept back into Galilee and the feeding of a multitude, substituting the ritual of the washing of the disciples' feet at the time of their final meal together. We cannot explore fully here the controversy over the nature of the Last Supper or the conflicting traditions as to its origin.[3]

But the Lord's Supper is the most distinctive aspect of Christian worship. Any attempt to attribute the Communion of the Lord's Supper in its origin to the developing later tradition stumbles at the point of Paul's clear acceptance of it as an already established element of the church's life and worship. So firmly embedded in the church was the Eucharist that a ritual had developed to which Paul could refer as set and rigid. The Synoptic phrases " This is my body " and the " blood of the covenant " are included by Paul (I Cor. 11:23-26). The practice of a communal meal and the relating of that meal to Jesus' meals with his disciples was a part of church life before Paul wrote what we now call the " Words of Institution " to the Corinthians. How far did he modify established procedures?

Whatever relationship this special meal bore to the ordinary " breaking of bread " by the Christians together is lost in ambiguity. Rudolf Bultmann distinguishes between the " breaking of bread " together and the Lord's Supper. He contends that the Christian meal celebrations of their fellowship became solemn occasions, the origin of which lay " without doubt in the table-fellowship which once had united Jesus and his ' disciples.' No special reference to Jesus' last meal was in them." These meal celebrations were Palestinian practice. According to Bultmann, it was in the Hellenistic congregations that the special references to the last meal of Jesus were observed. However, Bultmann quotes E. Lohmeyer, who, while also distinguishing two types of meals to be found in the early church, attributes the meal celebrations to the Galilean tradition and the remembrance of a Last Supper to the Jerusalem party.[4] Cullmann follows Lietzmann in discerning two conceptions of the Eucharistic meal in primitive Christianity but raises the obvious question as to " how the Apostle Paul could have had the audacious idea of establishing a relation between, on the one hand, this joyful feast of the first Christians and, on the other, the Last Supper with its close association with Jesus' death." [5] His answer is that Paul took the joyous meal celebrations of the early Christians, which were ordinary meals in which the risen Lord's presence was experienced and perceived, not only as a historical link " between the first meal of the Risen Lord and the last meal of the Man Jesus " but " an internal link " as well. That link is the Presence of Christ, and " in the Lord's Supper it is not only the Risen One who reveals Himself to the community but the Crucified One." [6]

These divergent views are cited to indicate the difficulty of being dogmatic in setting forth the origins of the Eucharist. We can affirm confidently that very early in the life of the church the breaking of bread and the sharing of wine in the context of congregational thanksgiving were intended to symbolize not only the resurrection but the crucifixion. Very early also these acts were intended as a commemoration of Jesus' final meal with his disciples. Paul's contribution to the developing tradition could not have been as revolutionary as some New Testament scholars would make it, for, at most, Paul modified or structured more plainly an already existing rite. Furthermore, it was a rite that rapidly came to be considered the supreme and unique act of Christian worship. There was nothing really comparable to it in orthodox Judaism. It was the mark of the church. By means of it the early Christians re-created the meaning of the First Advent of their Lord and anticipated his Second Advent.

Christian worship then, rooted in synagogue practices,

was influenced by the Temple tradition. It was distinctive from the beginning, especially at the point of its increasing emphasis upon its peculiar institution of the Lord's Supper. From the synagogue it gained a high view of the written tradition, first of Judaism as set forth in the Law and the Prophets, then of its own leaders as set down in their writings and in the Gospels that proclaimed the church's remembrance and faith in Jesus. They followed the synagogue practice of encouraging commentary on the portions of Scripture that were read. This forerunner of the sermon became increasingly important. Music, the Word read and spoken, prayers — these practices were basic. In addition, the peculiar and distinctively Christian sharing of the bread and wine in an increasingly liturgical setting, with fixed prayers and required language of institution, came to be central.

The awe and reverence with which the Eucharist was surrounded led to the practice of separating its liturgy from the remaining liturgy of the Word and the dismissal before the Sacrament was observed of those who had not been baptized. By the end of the second century the acts of worship of the primitive church were fairly well regularized and set into patterns. There was some variety within the general pattern and a degree of extemporaneous expression in prayer. The direction in which the Christian community moved was plain. It was toward formalization of the ritual of worship. Such a movement was inevitable as the church grew and as it developed into an institution of society. Protestants have tended to see in this development a waning of the pristine vigor and enthusiasm of the early Christians. Such a waning did occur but to attribute it to the regularization of worship is too facile an interpretation. Actually, such a regularization was not only inevitable, it was desirable. The traditions of the past are handed from one generation to another, in part through forms. A sense of history is maintained through forms and set patterns. As the stories of Jesus and as the interpretations of his meaning as understood by such early followers as Paul, Luke, " Matthew," " Mark," and the author of the Fourth Gospel were being regularized in a canon of Scripture, so the historical events of the life of Christ and their meaning were being structured into liturgical frameworks. Their meaning and foundation might well have been clouded had such a systematization not come about.

Clearly and unmistakably the Christians drew upon the Jewish background and procedures in corporate worship to celebrate the redemptive act of God in Christ their Lord. They made use of the familiar and at the same time infused it with the great glad tidings of the new covenant. Worship was a proclamation, not only of what had happened, but of what was happening within the community of those who could say, " Jesus is Lord."

CHAPTER 3

The Word and the Table

In 1875 a document known as the Didache or The Teaching of the Twelve Apostles was discovered at Constantinople. The exact date of its composition must remain unknown although it is generally accepted as being a product of the second century, probably of the period between A.D. 120 and 150. The Didache gives evidence of the fact that both a method of baptism, in cold running water preferably, and a formula, " in the name of the Father and of the Son and of the Holy Spirit," had been developed. There are also explicit directions in relation to the Eucharist.

Now about the Eucharist: This is how to give thanks: First in connection with the cup:
"We thank you, our Father, for the holy vine of David, your child, which you have revealed through Jesus, your child. To you be glory forever."
Then in connection with the piece [broken off the loaf]:
"We thank you, our Father, for the life and knowledge which you have revealed through Jesus, your child. To you be glory forever.
"As this piece [of bread] was scattered over the hills and then was brought together and made one, so let your Church be brought together from the ends of the earth into your Kingdom. For yours is the glory and the power through Jesus Christ forever."
You must not let anyone eat or drink of your Eucharist except those baptized in the Lord's name. For in reference to this the Lord said, " Do not give what is sacred to dogs."

After you have finished your meal, say grace in this way:

" We thank you, holy Father, for your sacred name which you have lodged in our hearts, and for the knowledge and faith and immortality which you have revealed through Jesus, your child. To you be glory forever.

" Almighty Master, ' you have created everything ' for the sake of your name, and have given men food and drink to enjoy that they may thank you. But to us you have given spiritual food and drink and eternal life through Jesus, your child.

" Above all, we thank you that you are mighty. To you be glory forever.

" Remember, Lord, your Church, to save it from all evil and to make it perfect by your love. Make it holy, ' and gather ' it ' together from the four winds ' into your Kingdom which you have made ready for it. For yours is the power and the glory forever."

" Let Grace come and let this world pass away."

" Hosanna to the God of David! "

" If anyone is holy, let him come.   If not, let him repent."

" Our Lord, come! "

" Amen."

In the case of prophets, however, you should let them give thanks in their own way.[1]

It is interesting to note that the prayers of thanksgiving in the offering of the cup and of the bread, as well as the concluding prayer " after you have finished your meal," are set forth with the direction, " This is how to give thanks." At the same time the cautionary note is added at the end that the prophets are not to be limited but are to be allowed to " give thanks in their own way." Although the liturgy of the Eucharist is assuming structure and regularity, there is still room for the spontaneity and even extemporaneity of the prophet.

The writings of Justin Martyr come from approximately the same period of the second century. Justin describes the assembling of the Christians for prayers and the reading of " the memoirs of the apostles or the writings of the prophets." [2] Following this, the president delivered a discourse, the congregation offered prayers, and the bread, the wine, and the water were brought for the Communion. No indication is given that the content of the prayers was fixed, but the formulas of procedure are plain. By the third century a detailed formulary had been evolved and was in use in the Roman Church, according to *The Apostolic Tradition of Hippolytus.* Hans Lietzmann offers the following translation of Hippolytus' liturgy:

Bishop: The Lord be with you.

Church: And with thy spirit.

Bishop: Lift up your hearts.

Church: We have them in the Lord.

Bishop: Let us give thanks to the Lord.

Church: That is proper and right.

Bishop: We thank Thee God through Thy beloved servant Jesus Christ whom Thou hast sent in the latter times to be our Savior and Redeemer and the messenger of Thy counsel, the Logos who went out from Thee, through whom Thou hast created all things, whom Thou wast pleased to send out from heaven into the womb of the Virgin, and in her body he became incarnate and shown to be Thy Son born of the Holy Ghost and of the Virgin. In order to fulfil Thy will and to make ready for Thee a holy people, he spread out his hands when he suffered in order that he might free from sufferings those who have reached faith in Thee.

And when he gave himself over to voluntary suffering, in order to destroy death, and to break the bonds of the devil, and to tread down hell, and to illuminate the righteous, and to set up the boundary stone, and to reveal the Resurrection, he took bread, gave thanks, and said: " Take, eat, this is my body which is broken for you." In the same manner also the cup, and said: " This is my blood which is poured out for you. As often as you do this you keep my memory."

When we remember his death and his resurrection in this way, we bring to Thee the bread and the cup, and give thanks to Thee, because Thou hast thought us worthy to stand before Thee and to serve Thee as priests.

And we beseech Thee that Thou wouldst send down Thy Holy Spirit on the sacrifice of the church. Unite them, and grant to all the saints who partake in the sacrifice, that they may

be filled with the Holy Spirit, that they may be strengthened in faith in the truth, in order that we may praise and
laud Thee through Thy servant, Jesus Christ, through whom
praise and honour be to Thee in Thy holy church now and
forever more, Amen.[3]

The third and fourth centuries provide us with a vastly
increased number of documents affording us information as
to the procedures and practices of the church in her worship. There are the writings of Clement of Alexandria, of
Ignatius, of Irenaeus, of Tertullian, of Origen, and of Cyril
of Jerusalem.[4] Certain common details begin to emerge
from an examination of these documents. For one thing, the
central place in worship is given to the Lord's Supper and
high reverence is attached to it. Although everyone is invited to the earlier parts of the worship, the unbaptized are
dismissed before the offering of the bread and wine. The
phrase *Ite, missa est* was pronounced by the presiding priest.
Thus the uninitiated are separated from the initiates for the
purpose of participation in the Communion.

Again, it may be noted, that the central responsibility of
a special vocational group in the leading of worship is evident. The deacons have significant functions, but the actual
prayers in connection with the Eucharist, the Fraction, and
the Elevation, are reserved for a celebrant who functions as
a priest on behalf of the congregation. This celebrant might
be a bishop responsible for a group of churches, for by this
time the office of bishop was clearly developed throughout
the church. The celebrant might be an elder, or more than
one elder acting in unison. He might be the chief elder, the
" presiding " elder or president of the congregation, as he is
sometimes called. The important thing to recognize is the
developing fact of a priesthood, a feature that the church of
the first century does not display. The role played by the
worshiping congregation is still a firsthand and vital one.
The Amens and Responses are for the most part congrega-
ional in nature. In a very real way worship is dialogue in
which leader and people share before God. Moreover, wor-

ship is corporate. It is not individualized in the way we so often find it in contemporary Protestantism. It is an act of the church, a deed of the congregation. When the celebrant acts alone he is still only representative, doing for the group what cannot be done by each person for himself as an individual.

The centrality of Scripture is obvious. Lessons from the lectionary included passages from the Law, the Prophets, the Epistles, The Acts, and the Gospels. Quite frequently the selections were long. There was no tendency to reduce the Scripture reading to six or eight verses, taken haphazardly from whatever place in Scripture suited the preacher's fancy or his sermon. Since the canon of Scripture was not yet fast, the letters of bishops and other church dignitaries were read with almost the same reverence as the Law, the Prophets, and the Epistles attributed to apostolic sources. However, supreme reverence was afforded the reading of the Gospels. " The people stood for the Gospel, as if hearing a proclamation from their king." [5] By the very act of standing, they symbolized their participation in the reading and hearing of the " proclamation from their king."

It may be noted, finally, that the worship procedures of the church were fairly rigidly structured by the fourth century. There was room for some variation, but the essential movement of the service was set. The prayer in connection with the Eucharist followed a pattern, progressing through notes of thanksgiving to the Words of Institution, after which was the recollection before God of the meaning of the Communion and then the petition for the coming of the Holy Spirit, and lastly the intercessions. Some extemporaneous prayers were allowed within the pattern, but for the most part the very words were definitely established.

The regularizing of the liturgy was not uniform throughout the church. The fifth and sixth centuries saw the development of clearly delineated families of rites. The main divisions were Eastern and Western. Each of these two primary rites was distinguished by subdivisions. In the

East three major types had been developed. They are known as the Alexandrian, the West Syrian, and the Byzantine. The Byzantine rite became the rite of the Orthodox Church, and with minor variations remains in use today. The sharp division between the Liturgy of the Catechumens and the Liturgy of the Faithful was marked in the East even after that division had become only a form in the West. The differences in liturgical mood and emphasis between East and West were already evident by the sixth century and have only been accentuated by the ensuing years. They include the atmosphere of mystery that pervades the Eastern rites. This sense of mystery was intensified by the practice of preparing the offertory of the Eucharist, which was no longer an offering of the people, behind a screen, with the congregation excluded.

The reverence that Christians felt for the proclamation of the gospel gave rise to the practice of the " Little Entrance " of the priest before the reading. The Gospel book was carried to the lectern and the ceremony was heightened until it involved a procession, lights, and the singing of hymns. The " Little Entrance " was, and is, a high point of Orthodox worship. The other high point was the " Great Entrance,"; when the elements of the Eucharist were brought in to be placed upon the altar. It was inevitable that such a service should become more and more a service in which the acts of worship were acts of the celebrant or celebrants. Although this is true in one sense, it is also true that the Eastern rite maintained a strong sense of corporateness. The congregation felt their participation in the Mystery. Their vocal share in the singing of hymns and responses and their silent share in the spiritual reality that was the mark of the Divine Presence kept the worship a vital emotional experience. Furthermore, the use of the vernacular made the acts of the celebrants intelligible. Communion was permitted in both elements. However, the elaboration of the element of the mysterious and the awesome began to discourage communication by the laity.

In the later liturgies, says T. S. Garrett, " there comes in a more gloomy and pessimistic emphasis as a result of the increased consciousness of sin and enhanced reverence in the presence of the great eucharistic mystery. Phrases such as ' thy lowly, sinful and unworthy slaves ' creep in, and at the Epiklesis, or invoking of the Holy Spirit, the Deacon says to the people: ' My beloved, how fearful is this moment and how dreadful is this time when the Holy Spirit descends from heaven, from the heights above, and dwells upon this Holy Qurbana (Eucharist) and sanctifies it ' (Syrian *Liturgy of St. James*). No wonder that the laity was afraid to approach the holy table and reception of communion declined." [6]

All in all, the developments in the East were marked by a great deal less variety than those in the West. By the eighth century, innovations ceased entirely, and the pattern of worship was completely rigid. Within that pattern, variations were not allowed. Thus the Eastern structure has remained. It is highly emotional, appealing to the feelings of the worshiper; highly symbolic, investing every act with pious significance; highly joyous, for all its emphasis on a consciousness of sin and the mystery of the Eucharist. Its joyous nature roots in its stress on the incarnation and on the Divine Presence of God through the Holy Spirit. The note of sacrifice that came to dominate the Western rite is subdued. God is in Christ, who is risen from the dead and who, by the Holy Spirit, dwells among us. Hallelujah!

George Hedley summarizes the general Eastern procedure:

It opens with a blessing and " the Great Litany," whose response is *Kyrie eleison*, " Lord, have mercy." There follow antiphons from the Psalms, alternating with hymns and sections of " the Little Litany." After the third antiphon, and with many introductory and concluding versicles, the " Apostle " (from the Acts or the epistles) and the Gospel for the day are read or chanted. With the sermon the period of instruction is ended, and the catechumens are dismisssed by the deacon's cry, " All ye learners, go out."

At the beginning of the Liturgy of the Faithful, the choir sings the Cherubic Hymn while the priest prays privately. Then he joins in the hymn, and in the "Great Entrance" brings the bread and wine in procession from the preparation table into the nave, and thence into the sanctuary by the central "holy doors." Another litany leads to the Nicene Creed, which in accordance with Eastern doctrine omits the *filioque*, "and from the Son." An "invitation to attend" concludes with the Grace (II Corinthians 13:14) and the *Sursum Corda*.

The Consecration begins with Preface ("It is meet and right") and *Sanctus* ("Holy, holy, holy"). The prayer itself is lengthy, and complicated with responses by the lesser clergy; but it is the same in essential structure as that of Hippolytus, and those that we know in the West. The most significant difference from Roman usage is the specific invocation of the Holy Spirit for the "changing of the holy things."

The saints, the departed, and the living faithful are commemorated, the Lord's Prayer is said, and the priest breaks the sacred disk into four parts and arranges it carefully on the paten. He and the other clergy then commune. What remains of the wafer is dropped into the chalice, and those who have prepared themselves to receive the Communion are given both kinds, "the Body and Blood together," in a spoon. A prayer of thanksgiving and one of dismissal bring the service to a close.[7]

There is majesty and grace in this ancient liturgy. The ecumenical movement has made it more familiar to Western Christendom today than it has been for centuries. For although the East was committed to the Byzantine rite, the West was developing in other directions with other emphases. The overall structure of all the liturgies was the same. All were rooted in the worship of the synagogue with the influence of the Temple in the background and the unique significance of the traditions that clustered around the Last Supper in the foreground. Cultural and environmental factors were operative. The sensuous mysteriousness of the Eastern culture is the atmosphere in which the Byzantine liturgy developed. The comparative stability of the East is to be detected in the early solidification of worship practices into more firmly set forms than the West was to attain for centuries. By the sixth century the Western Church had developed subfamilies as had the East, but no one of these divisions of liturgical types was to become dominant as early as the Byzantine rite had gained supremacy. In the West the main classifications were the Roman and the Gallican liturgies. They were clearly discernible by the end of the fifth century even though documentary evidence of procedures before A.D. 500 is fragmentary and incomplete.

CHAPTER 4

The Word Lost in Symbols

Within the Western Church by the end of the fifth century the Roman and Gallican rites existed side by side. The Roman liturgy, as its nomenclature would imply, was found in use in the city from which its name derived and in those areas of the church under Rome's influence. With the passing of time the growing dominance of the Roman Church led to an increasing use of the Roman ritual. At the beginning of the sixth century the Gallican rite was in use over far more widespread areas of the church than was the Roman rite. At the same time there was a great deal more variation in details within the general structure of the Gallican usages than within the Roman. Existing as they did side by side, each family of rites influenced the other so that by the time the Roman liturgy attained preeminence it had been distinctly modified by the rival liturgy. As Maxwell comments, " The Roman rite of the tenth century was not that of the fourth or fifth century, but one considerably altered by Gallican influence and containing much Gallican material." [1]

The origins of the Gallican rite are impossible to trace in detail. Actually, Dom Gregory Dix insists that there is no warrant for speaking of *the* Gallican rite as being distinctive of all the West, including Africa, while leaving the Roman ritual as an isolated expression of worship confined to the city and suburbs of Rome. The term should be confined to those rites used in what is now geographically France.[2] However, the term has been stretched to cover the rites used throughout most of Europe, and since there were distinctive characteristics in these usages which differentiate the liturgies of the Western Church as a whole from those churches which were under Roman influence, the term may be used to cover not only the strictly Gallican but the Ambrosian and Mozarabic as well. The Ambrosian, or Milanese liturgy, has been preserved until the present day in Milan. The Mozarabic liturgy persisted in Spain until the twelfth century. By special dispensation it was revived in the diocese of Toledo in the sixteenth century and has remained in use there.

It is impossible to trace in detail the early development of either the Roman or the Gallican rite. Somewhere in the late third or early fourth century the Greek rites of an early time began to appear in Latin. The Roman form seems complete in its general structure earlier than the Gallican, and it is possible to reproduce it as it was celebrated about the end of the fifth century.

Liturgy of the Word

Introit by two choirs as clergy enter
Kyries
Celebrant's salutation
Collect(s)
Prophecy or Old Testament lection
Antiphonal chant
Epistle
Gradual (Psalm sung originally by one voice)
Alleluia
Gospel, with lights, incense, responses
Dismissal of those not communicating (*Greg. Dialog.* I. ii. 23)

Liturgy of the Upper Room

Offertory: Collection of elements, spreading of corporal on altar, preparation of elements for communion, offering of gifts, admixture, psalm sung meanwhile
Salutation and *Sursum corda*

Prayer of Consecration:
  Preface
  Proper Preface
  Sanctus
  Canon
Kiss of Peace
Fraction
Lord's Prayer with protocol and embolism
Communion, celebrant first, then people (Psalm sung mean-
    while)
Post-communion collect (Thanksgiving)
Dismissal by deacon [8]

Dr. Maxwell makes a sharp division of the liturgy into
that of " Word " and of " Upper Room." It may be questioned whether so sharp a contrast is valid. Actually the
liturgy was one, divided into that to which all were invited
and that which was distinctively intended for the initiate
or baptized Christian. The stress in the earlier part of the
service was upon the Scriptures. The stress in the latter part
of the service was upon the Eucharist. Professor Hardman
designates the first part as " The Liturgy of the Catechumens " and the second part as " The Liturgy of the Faithful." [4] Dom Gregory Dix uses the term " Synaxis," or
" meeting," for the first part of the service and " Eucharist "
proper, or " thanksgiving," for the second part. The two
were separable, and each could be held without the other. [5]

The structure of the Liturgy of the Word (following
Maxwell's nomenclature) in both the Gallican and the
Roman rite is essentially the same, with the principal acts
in each centering upon the entry of the clergy and the reading of the Gospel. The use of lights, incense, and responses
at the time of the reading of the Gospel was a result of
Gallican influence and was not found in the more primitive
forms of the Roman rite. The Gallican ritual gave a place
to the sermon or homily that was often not found in the
Roman form even as early as the sixth century. In addition
there were longer prayers, a greater use of propers, and
more responses in the Gallican form. When we examine

the Liturgy of the Upper Room in these two developing families we see evidence of the more diffused and longer nature of the Gallican usages as over against the Roman. The number of collects and responses, of antiphons and symbolic acts, is plainly greater even upon a cursory comparison of the two orders. It is generally agreed that the Gallican form is more highly symbolic, more ornate and elaborate, more flamboyant and dramatic than the Roman. Its appeal to the senses is indicated by an elaborate use of incense and lights. By way of contrast, the Roman liturgy manifests characteristic Roman qualities of starkness and conciseness, of austerity and simplicity.

Such differences are relative only, and increasingly the Roman rite was influenced by the Gallican. However, it was the Roman liturgy, with Gallican alterations, that became the dominant usage in the Western Church. Essentially it remained Roman in form and, as compared with the Eastern ritual, was marked by terseness and economy, both in words and in symbolism. Less congregational participation was called for than in either the Eastern or the Gallican Mass. (The word " Mass," probably a corruption of the words of dismissal following the Liturgy of the Word, *Ite, missa est,* was used by Augustine and is regarded as a descriptive term in the records of the Councils of Carthage about A.D. 398.) As a result the worshipers tended to become spectators. The responses and other types of group participation were in process of becoming the prerogatives of the choir rather than acts of the congregation as a whole. The triumph of the Roman form of the Mass over the Gallican form carried with it the removal of the act of worship from the nave to the chancel to a degree that was to become one of the most significant features of the church life of the High Middle Ages.

Gradually the Gallican rite was fading from usage in the seventh and eighth centuries except in its Celtic form which prevailed in Ireland until well into the tenth century. The Roman rite, with its Gallican infusions, was losing its un-

adorned leanness and displaying a highly dramatized richness. The less corporate nature of worship and the increased
importance of the priesthood helped to create a situation
in which the spectacle would assume greater and greater
objective elements to appeal to the eyes of the viewing
congregation. In addition, the developing concept of transubstantiation played a major role in the objectivization
and the clericalizing of worship. The West had long
stressed the sacrificial aspect of the Eucharist. As the escha-
talogical hope faded completely and the church came to
terms with history, it did so in the Mass by looking back
to the death of Christ upon the cross and the reenactment
of that death upon its altars. The doctrine of the Eucharist
was gradually developing.

In the early centuries of the church there had been no
particular speculation as to the meaning of the presence of
Christ in the Eucharist. Consequently, no theories as to the
nature of that Presence were formulated. It was assumed
that the Presence was " real " but no one asked what " real "
meant. Both Ambrose and Augustine, two of the most influential Latin fathers of the church, had spoken in strong
terms of Christ's being in the bread upon the altar, but their
words had not implied any metaphysical change in the nature of the bread itself and were perfectly compatible with
a spiritual comprehension of a " Real Presence." John of
Damascus, writing during the middle of the eighth century,
had spoken of the " change " of the bread and wine in the
celebration of the Mass but had done so in very indefinite
terms.

It was Paschasius Radbertus who, in the ninth century,
published a treatise on *The Lord's Body and Blood,* the first
book by any author ever to be devoted to the Eucharist.[6]
Radbertus insisted that after the consecration the bread and
wine became identical with the natural body of Christ, the
very same body he inhabited on earth and now inhabits in
heaven. One of the monks in the abbey of which Radbertus
was abbot, Ratramnus of Corbie, refuted his superior's posi-

tion in the strongest possible terms. By the eleventh century the view espoused by Radbertus was so generally accepted that when Berengar of Tours in A.D. 1050 indicated his own acceptance of the position held by Ratramnus, he was excommunicated and restored only after refuting his heresy. Berengar, incidentally, continued to have trouble with the prevailing orthodoxy and was forced a second time in A.D. 1079 to profess adherence to the view that the consecration of the elements effected a " substantial " change into " the real flesh of Christ which was born of the Virgin." [7]

Whatever controversies might take place among scholars, the period between the eighth and tenth centuries saw widespread acceptance of a pragmatic doctrine of transubstantiation among the masses of the people. It was an age of general belief in miracles and of superstitious awe in the presence of any manifestations of the Holy. Appeal to the intelligence through preaching and through Scripture, even the verbal expressions of the congregation in prayer, lost their power before the miracle enacted anew upon the altars of the church by means of the formula of the Mass.

In accordance with the theology that had developed, the practice of the clergy underwent subtle but important modifications. The practice of pushing the altar back against the wall began in the tenth century. The custom of building the altar toward the east was an ancient one, apparently based upon the east as the source of light. Now the clergy began the practice of performing the Mass with backs to the congregation in the so-called Eastward Position. Although not intended to signify a gulf between the celebrating priests and the communing congregation, the practical effect of this custom came to indicate a gulf. All emphasis upon Communion was secondary. The fellowship of the Lord's Supper was no longer evident in the Mass, and the thought of the Eucharist as a congregational act was obscured. It was no longer important that the worshipers understand what was going on at the altar as the words of the Eucharist were spoken. So Latin, no longer intelligible to the masses of the people, was the language of the liturgy. Since they could not understand had they been able to hear, it was no longer necessary for the congregation to hear. The words were therefore mumbled by the priestly celebrant or uttered in so low a tone that only a few could distinguish them. These changes were not deliberate endeavors to exclude the congregation from the worship practices of the church. They were a part of the pattern of an age wherein ignorance and superstition were rampant. Actually, the devotional life of multitudes was nourished by attendance upon Mass and by participation at least as spectators. The low ebb of verbal communication is obviously reached in this era. Still faithful Christians followed the movement of the service as they observed the actions of the priest, heard the ringing of the bells, prayed the Pater Noster, and indulged in their private devotions.

The beginnings of individualism were here, however — an individualism that was to wreak havoc with the idea of the Eucharist as a corporate act. More and more the individual worshiper turned to his own devotional acts while the Mass was being said at the altar. In the actual service of the Eucharist he had no immediate part. It was a miracle performed for him by those who had been ordained for that purpose. In addition it was a miracle fraught with grave consequences to those who handled it unworthily or unwarily. A man might eat or drink damnation to his soul if he handled this very flesh of his Lord or the cup of his actual blood incautiously. As a result, the Christians of this age drew back from the Lord's Table. Only the priest communed regularly. The people of the parish for the most part communed only a few times a year, and finally, it became a universal custom to commune only at Easter. The church had moved away from the celebration of the Eucharist as an act of the congregation in which the celebrants functioned with and for the whole people. The Eucharist had now become a deed peculiar to the clergy, the benefits of which might be given to the people or withheld from them. The congregation looked on at what was done; they communed only occasionally.

The popularity of private Masses, and their abuse, was but another indication of the direction in which the worship practices of the church had moved. If the Mass was an act of the priest, who alone had the power to carry out the ritual on behalf of the whole congregation, why should not the same act be accomplished on behalf of individuals for individual benefit and at individual behest? The result was grave abuse. Private Masses were held for the dead (with consequent pecuniary involvements that led to the degradation of the Mass), for success in temporal affairs, for safety on journey, for changes in the weather. The Mass became an instrument for manipulating God for private ends. Masses were even said for the death of an enemy, although this practice was early condemned by the Council of Toledo in A.D. 694. The period prior to the tenth century in Europe was a culturally barren era, an intellectually empty, spiritually dry epoch of history.

The abuses in connection with the life and practice of the church were understandable if account is taken of the mental and religious destitution of the common people. The symbols of the Christian faith became ends in themselves, and to material symbols were attached magic properties by the popular mind. An illustration of this development is seen in the withdrawal from regular Communion by the vast majority of the people. When they did partake, the dread awe with which they regarded the elements is seen in the widespread custom of administering the bread by placing it in the communicant's mouth instead of in his hands. The denigration of preaching contributed to the situation, for the enlightenment that intelligent preaching affords being lacking, the laity were bereft of instruction in the meanings of the liturgy and in the historical aspects of the Christian faith. What preaching there was too frequently concerned itself with miraculous legends of the saints, with the growing extravagances concerning the Virgin Mary, and with an ethic that was discharged when attendance upon ecclesiastical duties was observed.

The Church of the West was at its low ebb, and the heart of its failure was at the point of worship. The vigor and beauty of Christian symbolism had been encased in a wooden literalism. When symbols become literal, they become objects of superstition. This is equally true of a crucifix or of the words of the Bible. Perhaps the historical forces whereby Christianity had spread so rapidly among so many diverse cultures made such a situation inevitable. The fact remains that worship reached its nadir as a meaningful experience in the ninth and tenth centuries.

CHAPTER 5

The Table Becomes the Altar

Changes in Europe in the eleventh and twelfth centuries brought changes in the church. Western culture began to stir. The church began to move toward the zenith of her secular and political power. This power reached its height in the thirteenth century, began its slow decline in the fourteenth century, and reached the crashing fragmentation of the Protestant Reformation in the sixteenth century. But by the eleventh century the worship practices of the church had so solidified that no further changes of importance were to take place within the West until the Reformation. Worship itself was an instrument of power. The unquestioned dominance of the cleric at the altar gave him authority to offer or withhold salvation from the suppliant. So generally was the miracle of transubstantiation accepted that no important voice was raised to recapture the idea of the Eucharist as a function of the whole church, including the laity, rather than as a clerical prerogative. The congregation now was almost solely a collection of spectators.

There were several ways of celebrating the Mass. The High Mass was a sung Mass requiring a priest assisted by a deacon, a subdeacon, servers, and a choir. When celebrated by a bishop assisted by priests, it was (and is, for the forms of the Mass are the same today) called a pontifical High Mass. A second, and increasingly popular, form was the Low Mass. This was an abridged form of High Mass, conducted without a choir by one priest and one or more servers. Since Communion by the people at High Mass was rare while it was usual at Low Mass, the continued popularity of this form of the Eucharist is understandable. In addition the curtailment of ceremonial made it far less time-consuming. A variation of Low Mass occurs when there are no servers to assist the priest and when the choir sings the parts of the service in their place. During the Middle Ages the occasional observance of Dry Mass arose in which the Low Mass was said or sung without actual consecration of the elements and without communication by either priests or people. Maxwell believes the Dry Mass to be important because " it proves to be not unlike the Ante-Communion in the Anglican Church and the Sunday Morning Service of the Reformed Church." [1] Perhaps even closer again to the Protestant services of the future was the Prone, which was a service in the vernacular consisting of prayers, Scripture, the Nicene Creed, a sermon or exhortation, and the Lord's Prayer.

The Mass was the worship center of the life of the medieval church. Although certain ceremonials differed in the three types of the Mass mentioned above, and while the musical accompaniment, or lack of it, varied, the Canons of the Mass did not differ in any essential. The theological view of the Mass as a reenactment of the sacrifice of our Lord to the practical exclusion of other significant aspects of the Eucharist; the loss of a sense of the corporate nature of the Eucharist as an act of the church and the corresponding tendency to make the high act of worship a clerical deed with the laity in a spectator role; the abuse of the symbols of the faith so that they tended in the popular mind to become reality rather than to point to reality; the increasing individualism created by the encouragement of the practice of indulging in private devotions while the sacrifice of the Mass was being enacted at the altar: these were features of the worship life of the church of the twelfth and thirteenth centuries that contained the seeds of dissolution of spiritual vitality. Although the church reached the apex of her influence in the political life of Europe in this period, her energies were sapped by a failure to maintain vitality in worship. The multiplication of ceremony occurred. Whereas the sixth-century liturgy contained approximately thirty separate items, the High Mass of the late medieval period contained nearly one hundred. All the while the active participation of the congregation was decreasing. Even the congregational responses in the movements of the Mass were primarily the function of the choirs and the assistants to the celebrant.

The architecture of the period reflected the changed concepts. Until the twelfth century a Romanesque style of building had prevailed in the West, a modification of the basilican form. The Gothic structures that arose in the twelfth, thirteenth, and fourteenth centuries were perfect expressions of the worship practices of the church. Theologically the soaring spires and vast arching ceilings bespoke the mystery and majesty of God. Will Durant calls Gothic architecture " the supreme achievement of the medieval soul " and " the greatest triumph of form over matter in all the history of art." [2] One can feel the force of these tributes, and standing before the art and architecture of medieval man, " forget the superstition and squalor, the petty wars and monstrous crimes, of the age of Faith; [and] marvel again at the patience, taste, and devotion of our medieval ancestors; [and] thank a million forgotten men for redeeming the blood of history with the sacrament of art." [3] When tribute has been paid and thanks have been given, the meaning of the Gothic cathedral in the developments of Christian worship remains. That meaning is found in the way in which the Mass as a performance by the clergy apart from the people had reached its culmination. The long nave was suitable for large crowds who might stand and watch. All lines of visual aid converged on the chancel and its altar. Audibility was poor, for, since much of the liturgy was said in inaudible tones and since it was in the Latin tongue, why should acoustics be a factor in design? The cathedral was a perfect artistic expression of the worship practices of the medieval church.

Donald Baillie quotes some words of Karl Barth's on the " genius and failure " of the Mass: " ' The mass in its conception, content and construction is a religious masterpiece. It is the highwater mark in the development of the history of religion and admits of no rival.' But then he goes on to say that that is just what is wrong with it. ' Religion with its masterpieces is one thing, Christian faith is another.' " [4] Barth is much too sweeping in his condemnation. His implication that it is necessary to strip the drama, the pageantry, the ceremonial, from the rites of the church in order to recapture the pristine purity of early Christianity is too harsh. The Middle Ages was a period of drama, of pageantry, of ceremony. At the same time in these emphatic words Barth highlights the dangers to which the life of the church was exposed. Its celebration of a " religious masterpiece " overshadowed its mediation of the Christian faith. One example is seen in the worship of the Host. The elements of the Sacrament were to be adored because they were the body of God. Thus God became localized, and magical powers were ascribed to the consecrated element outside of the Eucharistic service itself.

Not all the leaders of the church were willing to accept the extreme views of popular devotion. Wycliffe protested against the worship of the Host a full century before the Reformation. " They are worse than heathens, believing that the consecrated host is their god," he wrote in De Eucharistia.[5] Popular piety reflects at last what the worship of the church projects through her rites and ritual. Theology is mediated to the laity primarily through worship. Belief is expressed in liturgy. Therefore, it follows that the average man's understanding of the nature of the Christian faith was distorted and perverted. When reformation came, it had to begin at the point of worship procedures. The symbols and practices of the church had to be evaluated anew, infused with new understanding, changed where distortion was so inherent as to be inevitable.

The doctrine of transubstantiation which had been widely held throughout the church since the eighth century was officially defined by the Fourth Lateran Council in A.D. 1215. " The practical outcome of this," writes Oscar Hardman, " was the multiplication of Masses for the benefit of the living and the dead. It became a general rule for all priests to say Mass daily, and numerous chapels and altars were provided in the larger churches in order to meet their need." [6] Other consequences in practice followed, as Hardman points out.[7] The elevation of the Host above the priest's head following the consecration, attended by the ringing of a bell, became universal. At first only the bread was so elevated but in the fourteenth century the practice of the elevation of the chalice followed. Adoration naturally came to be given to the elements that were not consumed in the Mass but reserved. The twelfth century also saw the beginning of the custom of withholding the chalice from the laity. The kiss of peace, a Jewish custom observed in the early church as a mark of fellowship and only infrequently indulged in after the first few centuries of Christianity, was now given to a paten or to a sacred object that was passed around the congregation. The increasing objectivization of worship left its mark everywhere upon the services of the church and reached a climax in the late fifteenth century on the eve of the Protestant Reformation. Both public and private devotions centered in symbols, verbal or otherwise, which were no longer means of expression for most Christians, but ends in themselves. As such they did not speak to the needs of the people at that deep level to which significant symbols must speak. The church met only the surface needs of many of her people.

An age was ending, a period of history was drawing to a close. Europe was changing. Her geographical frontiers were being pushed out. The Crusades had begun this process and then " in 1492 Columbus sailed the ocean blue." Europe's economic life was in process of transition. The feudal age was decaying, waving fading banners in dying hands. A commercial society with a bourgeois class was forming in the growing cities. With the growth of the cities and the bourgeois went a growth in nationalistic fervor. Princes, kings, and lesser rulers grew restive under the domination of a Roman pope. The Latin liturgies of a Roman church did not speak in the way they had once spoken to the German who was very conscious of his German language and the Englishman very conscious of his Anglo-Saxon tongue. Most important was the intellectual Renaissance. The church was not speaking to the intellectual of the fourteenth and fifteenth centuries. Her symbols did not convey meaning. When symbols do not reach the poets, artists, and scholars who are the cutting edge of culture, they will eventually lose their power to influence society. Widespread skepticism was characteristic of the world of the scholar. Although most of Europe's intelligentsia held to the outward forms of the church, multitudes of them no longer were held by the inner meaning.

The reaction of the church to the restlessness abroad was an ever greater rigidity. When symbols become empty, there is the tendency to increase the demand for at least outward acceptance of them. There is also the tendency to refuse to countenance examination or change. There were few changes in the liturgy of the church in the late Middle Ages and what changes there were proceeded " mainly from a desire to emphasize and explain certain gestures. Eucharistic theology, on the contrary, advanced to the settlement of debated questions and to the conclusion of a long-continued process of developing opinion by the formulation of exact interpretations of the essential mystery and primary use of the sacrament." [8]

Apart from the Mass, there is little to be said regarding public worship in this period, for the Mass was public worship. Preaching fluctuated in its power. The early Middle Ages found preaching at an extremely low ebb. A revival took place in the twelfth century, a revival that spent itself by the late thirteenth century. Dargan comments: " When we compare the preaching of the thirteenth century with that of two other culminating periods — the fourth and the sixteenth — which preceded and followed it, we shall find that in respect of real Biblical content and sound evangelical character, it falls immeasurably below them. It was a sadly distorted gospel which was preached in the thirteenth century." [9] The same history declares that " the state of the Catholic pulpit during the fourteenth and fifteenth century may be comprehensively and accurately described as one of decay." [10] It is true that voices of reform were beginning to be heard in the church. There was John Wycliffe in the fourteenth century and John Hus late in the same century. A hundred years later the voice of John Colet was heard in England about the same time that the incomparable and paradoxical Savonarola was thundering in Florence. These exceptions do not destroy the generalization that Christian preaching was at its lowest ebb in the two centuries before the Reformation.

No survey covering the period encompassing the eleventh and twelfth centuries can ignore, however, the vital contributions made to the spiritual life of the church by the monastic orders. Surely meaningful and creative worship is not lacking in an age that produced the Cistercian Order, the revival among the Benedictines, and the deepening vigor of the choir offices in the monasteries. These devotional services which had originated in the sixth and seventh centuries were related to the hours of the day. They were based upon the Psalter and the reading of the Bible. Hymns were later added. Protestantism is enriched still by the Anglican morning and evening prayers based upon the choir offices of the monasteries. Nor was individual piety lacking. The crucifix came into common use in the. eleventh century as a reminder of the sacrifice of our Lord. Popular piety clustered around its symbolism. The use of the rosary became widespread through the influence of the Dominicans in the thirteenth century. The use of the Ave Maria also arose in the thirteenth century. The ringing of the Angelus was a reminder of the annunciation and in response the Ave Maria was recited as an act of personal devotion. The laity possessed a prayer book, the Book of Hours, to which the devout turned for appropriate acts of worship at regular times. There was little room for spontaneity. Private devotion like public worship was rather rigidly structured, but there was room within the structure for true praise and worthy adoration. It must be remembered that this was not an age in which general creativity might be expected. Ignorance was widespread, superstition was rampant, illiteracy was general. It may well be argued that the only possible vehicles for conveying the essentials of the Christian heritage from one generation to the next were rigidly structured ones.

As the Middle Ages drew to a close new factors in every area of European culture were operative, pounding away at the public institutions and changing the social complexion of the entire Continent. Slowly but surely, changes were taking place, and the Europe of the late fourteenth and early fifteenth centuries was not the Europe of the eleventh and twelfth centuries.

At the end of the fifteenth century, Europe was in confusion and in flux. Religiously, the decay was widespread. It was an age of symbols that no longer conveyed reality to the extent they once had. As the Continent made its transition into a new era of history, intellectually, geographically, politically, economically, and socially, it also began the transition religiously. Christianity was far from dead or dying. The faith of the church was so embedded in the culture consciousness of the West that the new age would have died aborning apart from Christianity. Philosophy, science, the literature of the next few centuries, all were rooted in Christian world views. Conduct and behavior were inseparably united with Christian values. Popular piety continued to maintain itself upon the old usages and symbols. Yet at the point of the church's thrust into society and her encounter with men in her sanctuaries, she did not speak in words and deeds expressive of the new age. She confronted the sixteenth century with symbols from another age. This in itself is not necessarily futile, for the symbols of the past may well be the symbols most vital to the present. However, they must speak to the present. This may require reinterpretation, new emphases, fresh modifications, the holding forth of continuing truths that exist behind old symbols. These things the Roman Church failed to achieve, and a resuscitation of the Christian gospel in terms relevant and vigorous was required. Thus the Protestant Reformation became inevitable.

CHAPTER 6

The Word and the Reformation

The climax of medieval worship was High Mass. This rite as practiced in the Western church on the eve of the Reformation and finally regularized in 1570, following the Council of Trent, is reproduced by Professor Maxwell as follows:

The Liturgy of the Word

Introit and
Kyrie eleison (ninefold) } sung by choir
    Entry of ministers
    Private preparation of ministers at altar steps (said secretly):
        Invocation, *In nomine Patris* . . .
        Ps. XLIII, with v. 4 as antiphon, and *Gloria*
        Ps. CXXIV. 8
        Confiteor and *Misereatur* of celebrant to ministers
        Confiteor and *Misereatur* of ministers to celebrant
        Versicles and response from psalms
        Collects *Aufer a nobis* and *Oramus te*
        Blessing of incense, and censing of altar and ministers
Gloria in excelsis said secretly by celebrant and sung by choir
Salutations and collects of the day, after which celebrant says
        the Epistle and gradual silently
Epistle, sung by subdeacon; response, *Deo gratias*
Gradual sung by choir
Tract or Sequence (if any) sung by choir, while are said
    Prayers and Preparation for the Gospel:
        Munda cor meum
        Jube Domine benedicere
        Dominus sit in corde tuo

Salutation, announcement of Gospel and ⎫
minister's response, *Gloria tibi Domine* ⎮ by celebrant
Gospel recited in low tone ⎮
Response by ministers, *Laus tibi Christe* ⎭
The same repeated, except for celebrant's blessing added,
    by deacon
Gospel, with lights and incense, sung by deacon, and responses
    sung by ministers
Preacher goes to pulpit:
    Intimations
    Bidding Prayers
    Epistle and Gospel read in vernacular
    Sermon
Nicene Creed sung as *Gloria in excelsis*
Salutation and bidding to prayer, but no prayer

The Liturgy of the Upper Room

Offertory: Psalm verses sung throughout while celebrant pro-
    ceeds secretly
    Offering of bread: collect, *Suscipe sancte Pater*
    Admixture of water to wine: collect, *Deus qui humanae*
    Offering of chalice: collect, *Offerimus tibi*
    Prayers, *In spiritu humilitatis* and *Veni sanctificator*
    Blessing of incense: *Per intercessionem*
    Censing of elements: *Incensum istud*
    Censing of altar, saying Ps. CXLI. 2-4
    Censing of ministers
    Washing of celebrant's hands, while he recites the *Lavabo*,
        Ps. XXV. 6-12, with *Gloria*
    Oblation, *Suscipe sancta Trinitas*, *Orate fratres* (said audi-
        bly) and *Suscipiat Dominus*
Secrets (collects corresponding to those of the day)
Salutation and *Sursum corda* (sung)
Prayer of Consecration:
    Preface and Proper Preface — sung by celebrant (then *Sanc-
        tus* and *Benedictus* said audibly)
    Sanctus, sung by choir while the celebrant proceeds with
        the Canon, said silently (except for raising of the voice
        at *Nobis quoque*), bell rung to announce beginning
    Elevation, with bells and incense at Words of Institution
        and singing of *Benedictus qui venit*
    Canon concludes with ecphonesis
Lord's Prayer sung by celebrant, with protocol and embolism
Pax and Fraction and Commixture

Agnus Dei said by celebrant, then sung by choir
Celebrant's Communion (while *Agnus Dei* is sung):
  Collect, *Domine Jesu Christe*
  Kiss of Peace to clergy
  Collects, *Domine Jesu Christe fili Dei vivi* and *Perceptio Corporis tui* and Centurion's words, *Domine non sum dignus* (said audibly)
  He receives the Bread, saying Words of Delivery
  Thanksgiving, Ps. CXVI. 12-13
  He receives the Cup, saying Words of Delivery
(Communion of the people, in one kind, with *Ecce Agnus Dei*, Words of Delivery and *Domine non sum dignus*: very rare at High mass)
Communion Psalm sung by choir
  Cleansing of chalice
  Collects *Quod ore sumpsimus* and *Corpus tuum Domine*
  Covering of Chalice
Salutation and Post-communion collects
Deacon's salutation and dismissal of people
Collect, *Placeat tibi*
Blessing of People, *Benedicat vos*
Last Gospel, John 1:1-14 and response *Deo gratias* [1]

A comparison of this order with the fourth-century Eucharist will indicate the extensive elaborations that had taken place. The private preparation and secret chants and prayers of the celebrant give evidence of the extent to which the Mass had become the prerogative of the priest rather than the privilege of the congregation.

The reform in worship that was so salient a feature of the total reform of the church occasioned by the Protestant movement was uneven. Essentially this was because of the pragmatic nature of the Reformation movement. It was not a systematic, monolithic evaluation of church life, with a consequent systematic program of reform. Some things were obvious: transubstantiation was the doctrine that underlay certain features of the Mass and with the repudiation of transubstantiation these features must go. The withholding of the cup from the laity was part of the system based upon the Roman view of the Mass that must also be repudiated. The elevation of the Host and the adoration thereof were gestures plainly related to the concept of transubstantiation, and must be eliminated, although Luther himself retained the elevation. The vernacular was introduced, and the audibility of the words of the celebrant was quickly required.

Other emphases were seen clearly by Luther as necessary qualities in the direction of the restoration of worship as a congregational act. The Word was to be read and spoken for the understanding of the people. Luther's Scripture-centered reform demanded this change. His idea of congregational participation led to the introduction of the singing of hymns by all the people and their share in the responses formerly the prerogative of choirs. Luther never ceased to use the term " Mass " for the Lord's Supper, but he reintroduced the idea of fellowship and emphasized it. The importance of the Mass was stressed, and Luther at first insisted upon its daily observance, but later modified this requirement to weekly celebration. Never did he push Communion out to the fringes of the church's worship as the later Reformers were to do.

Luther scaled the worship service of the church down to the following revision:

Liturgy of the Word
Introit or German hymn
Kyrie eleison
Salutation and collect
Epistle
German hymn
Gospel
Apostles' Creed (Elements prepared now)
Sermon or homily

Liturgy of the Upper Room
Paraphrase of the Lord's Prayer
Exhortation
Recitation of Words of Institution, accompanied by
    Fraction and Delivery
Communion, hymns sung meanwhile
Post-communion collect
Aaronic Blessing [2]

A comparison of this simple service with that reproduced at the beginning of the chapter shows the far-reaching nature of Luther's reform in worship. Yet, Martin Luther was a reluctant Reformer in many aspects of his work. He did not cast the Latin Mass aside entirely, but retained it for certain feast days of the Christian calendar. He retained the use of vestments, of lights, of shrines and pictures, of crucifixes and bells. The Communion table remained an altar and Luther served from the Eastward Position. His principle in relation to worship procedures was a simple but very important one: Whatever is not forbidden by Scripture is allowed if in the judgment of the church it is helpful. His substitution of the doctrine of consubstantiation for that of transubstantiation has seemed to many a not very clear-cut reinterpretation of the meaning of the Mass. However, it contained a very significant and revolutionary principle. It was the principle that although the Real Presence was manifest in the bread and wine, this Presence could not be realized except as the worshiper partook of the elements. Thus the laity were drawn back into the completed act of Communion. It was not a miracle performed by the priest apart from the people. It was a realized and completed miracle only when the people participated in it by receiving the consecrated elements.

What is the sacrament of the Altar? It is the true body and blood of our Lord Jesus Christ, under the bread and wine, instituted by Christ himself for us Christians to eat and drink. Where is this written? The holy Evangelists, Matthew, Mark and Luke, together with St. Paul, write thus: "Our Lord Jesus Christ, in the night in which he was betrayed, took bread; and when he had given thanks, he brake it, and gave it to his disciples, saying, Take, eat; this is my body, which is given for you; this do in remembrance of me. After the same manner, when he had supped, he took also the cup, and when he had given thanks, he gave it to them, saying, Drink ye all of it; this cup is the New Testament in my blood, which is shed for you, for the remission of sins; this do, as oft as ye drink it, in remembrance of me." What benefit is such eating and drinking? It is shown us by these words: " Given and shed for you, for the remission of sins"; namely, that in the Sacrament, forgiveness of sins, life and salvation are given us through these words. For where there is forgiveness of sins, there is also life and salvation. How can bodily eating and drinking do such great things? It is not the eating and drinking indeed that does it, but the words which stand here: "Given and shed for you, for the remission of sins." These words, together with the bodily eating and drinking, are the chief thing in the Sacrament; and he that believes these words, has what they say and mean, namely the forgiveness of sins.[3]

Thus Luther roots the meaning of the Eucharist in response to words of Scripture which bespeak the living Word, Christ himself. The Mass, according to this view, does not create God, as popular thought loosely interpreted the theology of the medieval church; it reveals God in Christ. On another occasion Luther wrote: "The holy sacrament of the altar, or of the holy and true body of Christ, has three parts which it is necessary for us to know. The first is the sacrament, or sign, the second is the significance of this sacrament, the third is the faith required by both of these; the three parts which must be found in every sacrament. The sacrament must be external and visible, and have some material form; the significance must be internal and spiritual, within the spirit of man; faith must apply and use both of these." [4]

Luther insisted on the Real Presence, but it was a Presence that involved faith for its "Real-ness" to become effectual in the life of the believer. Furthermore, the community was involved. Although Luther plainly taught the individual's responsibility before God, he did not teach individualism divorced from community. "The significance or purpose of this sacrament is the fellowship of all saints, whence it derives its common name *synaxis* or *communio*, that is, fellowship; and *communicare* means to take part in this fellowship, or as we say, to go to the sacrament, because Christ and all saints are one spiritual body, just as the inhabitants of a city are one community and body, each citizen being a member of the other and a member of the entire city." [5] Luther's further insistence upon the involvement of the congregation through the use of the vernacular (though not always), through the requirement that the words of the celebrant be audible, and through the use of congregational hymns was revolutionary in its implications. Worship was again the act of the church with ministers as priests acting with and on behalf of the entire congregation. However, symbols and customs that had grown up through the years remained in use where Luther's influence dominated. This was not true of the Zwinglian reform.

Huldreich Zwingli was a child of the Renaissance as well as a child of the Reformation. He showed little of Luther's medievalism of mind and spirit. He displayed little sense of the mystical. His approach to religion was rational and in his concept of worship his ideals were simplicity and moral reality. Whereas Luther moved slowly in his revisions of the Mass, Zwingli moved quickly. He did not consider it the norm of worship, believing that four times a year was enough for its celebration. He stressed the memorial aspect of the Lord's Supper. When it was observed by Zwingli in the church at Zurich, the Supper was stripped to bare essentials. There was no prayer of consecration or intercession. It was Zwingli who introduced the custom of sitting, rather than kneeling, for the reception of the elements. Zwingli completely rejected the doctrine of transubstantiation and with almost equal vigor rejected Luther's doctrine of consubstantiation. The Reformation shattered on a theological issue involving worship practices when, at the Marburg Colloquy in 1529, Zwingli argued that the words, "This is my body," were to be understood only as a metaphor and not in any literal sense whatsoever. Luther with great vehemence argued to the contrary and sought an agreement on the basis of the Real Presence. Philip Melanchthon was helpless to mediate the two positions. At last Luther angrily rejected the hand that Zwingli, with tears in his eyes, extended and he stalked from the room, flinging over his shoulder words of anathema. Roland Bainton declares that though a common confession based on agreement as to the nature of the Lord's Supper failed, Luther momentarily agreed to the idea that intercommunion be practiced. However, Melanchthon, fearful of the reaction of the emperor and of Ferdinand of Austria, interposed. This " means," says Bainton, " that Luther did not play the role of utter implacability commonly ascribed to him, and was disposed to join with the Swiss until Melanchthon made him aware that to coalesce with the left would estrange the right." [6] Regardless of whose was the responsibility, the burgeoning Protestant movement in its two principal strongholds, Switzerland and Germany, was disrupted in worship. Failure in intercommunion meant failure in unity, the same failure that affords glaring evidence to the world at every ecumenical gathering of the fact that we are not one in Christ.

Zwingli's view of the Mass was not the only point at which he was influenced in his views on worship by his humanist background. His approach was rationalistic to the point that nearly all symbols save verbal ones were rejected. The Zurich services were didactic in the extreme. Though he himself was a lover of music and deeply appreciative of it as an art, Zwingli abolished all music from the services of the church. A normal Sunday service in Zurich consisted of:

A Prayer
Sermon (Expository in form and didactic in content)
Confession and absolution
Prayer and Benediction

Even the prayers were pedantic, partaking little of praise and containing almost no petition. Zwingli's rationalism led to a rejection of the sensuous and the mystical. He felt that none of the arts contributed anything whatsoever to the religious life of the Christian. Not only music but painting and sculpture were to be eliminated as aids to worship. Luther had a far wider appreciation than Zwingli of the total appeal of worship. However, it was the barer, more austere Zwinglian asceticism that was to dominate most of Protestantism in its relation to architecture, the visual arts, and music. Zwinglian rationalism also underscored the subjective individualism that had become a feature of the late Middle Ages. As the individual was encouraged in the use of private devotional aids, even during the celebration of the Mass, the importance of his subjective feelings was increased. Catholicism allowed him to retain objective aids, but Zwinglianism stripped him even of these. He was thus left with " faith," a faith that rested upon his feeling of response to the instruction of the Scriptures. This instruction came about largely by the laying of mind against mind as the minister read and interpreted the Bible. The other facets of communication involving the senses and the emotions were ignored. Worship in the Zwinglian tradition became stark, bereft of medieval richness and wholeness.

Although neither Luther nor Zwingli conceived the thrust of the Reformation to be at the point of worship, this is exactly where it lay. The Christian faith meets the people in worship. When worship procedures are vital, and convey valid and meaningful theological insights, the faith comes alive in the hearts of the worshipers. Failure in worship to mediate the gospel was characteristic of late medieval Christianity. The ability of the Reformers to make fresh and relevant the worship practices of the church spelled success for the Reformation movement. However, neither Luther nor Zwingli nor the other Reformers, for that matter, perceived this fact in the abstract. They sensed it pragmatically. Luther, for example, was aware of the need for involving the congregation in an experience whereby theological principles such as justification by faith and the priesthood of believers might become real. He therefore involved his people in worship that included the use of the vernacular, the partaking in both kinds of the elements, and the singing of hymns. Zwingli, influenced by the Renaissance, brought his rationalistic principles to bear and highlighted verbal and intellectual images as vehicles of worship. In Zwingli is to be found the opposite extreme from the highly sensuous, highly dramatic, mystical Mass that had spoken to the highly sensuous, highly dramatic, superstitious age of feudalism. A new era was in process of coming into being. Both Zwingli and Luther contributed to the life of the church as she began to speak in different voices to that era.

CHAPTER 7

The Word Among the Calvinists

The Reformation was a revolution in worship led by men who had little information that could carry them back beyond the practices of the church they knew to an appreciation of the developing history of the church's worship. Yet to an amazing degree they sensed the symbols that most adequately conveyed Christian truth to their age. The church spoke with new relevance. Some of the leaders of the Reformation movement discarded more of the heritage of the past than did others. Their efforts were experimental and the results in practice, as we have already seen in Zwingli and Luther, were vastly different. They approached the worship life of the church from the standpoint of theological emphases. Luther revived the sense of individual responsibility with his insistence on the centrality of justification by faith. At the same time he renewed the life of community in the Eucharist as an expression of the priesthood of believers. The community in Christ made all men who were believers in him ministers and, therefore, all were to be participants in the worship acts of the church. Zwingli brought to the fore the importance of instruction and exhortation, the communication of truth in a form that could be grasped by an understanding faith. Writing of the changes in the life of the church during the sixteenth century, Professor Maxwell states that " the most serious defect lay in the fact that the continental Reformers were without any profound historical knowledge of the origins and principles of worship. Their acquaintance with liturgical forms appears to have been largely restricted to the contemporary Roman forms; of Gallican and Eastern worship they appear to have known almost nothing; and their knowledge of even the primitive worship that they wished to restore was rudimentary and incomplete." [1] If this is true, it is astonishing that they combined the needs of their age with the essence of the gospel message as well as they did.

As we turn to an examination of the development of the liturgies of the Calvinistic tradition, we note that there is in them less of the reluctance of Luther toward change and less of the sweeping radicalism of Zwingli. But before we deal with Calvin himself it is necessary to look at the Reformation in Strasbourg. For Strasbourg lies behind Geneva and, says Jones, " Some of the most significant work pertaining to reformed worship took place at Strasbourg." [2] It was 1526 before Luther overcame his hesitancy and published a German Mass. Diobald Schwarz, of Strasbourg, had used an adaptation of the Roman rite in German in 1524. Schwarz's adaptation was printed immediately, and the Strasbourg influence on the development of Protestant liturgies was to be felt from then until the work of Schwarz and his successors was merged into the Calvinist tradition. Martin Bucer's influence upon Schwarz's work moved it in the direction of further simplification and toward more Protestant features such as a choice in the Creed (the Apostles' Creed might be used instead of the Nicene), a choice in prayers, a simplification of the ceremonial with elimination of the elevation of the Host, and a basilican as opposed to an Eastward Position for the celebrant of the Lord's Supper.

It was Bucer who substituted the title " Lord's Supper " for the Eucharist in place of " Mass." He also introduced the Protestant term " minister " for " priest " and " altar table " and finally " table " for " altar." All of the saints days were abolished, and the Eucharistic vestments were discarded at Strasbourg in favor of a black gown with cassock. Like Luther, Bucer was an advocate of congregational singing, and both metrical psalms and hymns were introduced into the service. Communion continued to be observed every Sunday. Bucer, by eliminating the lesson from the epistle and using a Gospel lesson only as the " crown of all Scripture," disapproved the use of the lectionary and, says Bard Thompson, " that method cost the church of Strasbourg its association with the Christian year; only the chief festivals were any longer observed." [3]

One of Bucer's basic principles in relation to the liturgy was his insistence upon Christian liberty, an insistence that grew out of his emphasis upon " the presence and inspiration of the Holy Spirit among those who worshipped. ' Except for the sermon,' he counselled, ' nothing should be dictated in the assembled congregation. Everyone may pray and praise without restraint.' " [4] Here was a new concept and one that in the centuries to come was to have great influence in breaking down order and regularity of procedure in worship. Bucer himself maintained this principle within the framework of a liturgy that, while greatly simplified, retained the overall structure of the Mass. His own description of the worship at Strasbourg goes as follows:

When the congregation come together on Sunday, the minister exhorts the people to confess their sins and to pray for pardon; and on behalf of the whole congregation he makes confession to God, prays for pardon, and pronounces absolution to the believers. Thereupon, the whole congregation sing a few short psalms or hymns. Then the minister says a short prayer, reads to the congregation a passage from the writings of the Apostles, and, as briefly as possible, expounds the same. Then the congregation sings again, this time the Ten Commandments, or something else. After that, the minister reads the Gospel, and preaches the sermon proper. The sermon ended, the congregation sing the Articles of our Belief [i.e., the Apostles' Creed in metre]; and the minister says a prayer for the Magistrates and for all men, and specially for the congregation there present, beseeching an increase of faith, love, and grace to hold in reverence the memory of Christ's death. Then he admonishes those who wish to observe the Lord's Supper with him that they are to do so in memory of Christ, to die to their sins, and bear their cross willingly, and be strengthened in faith for what must come to pass when we contemplate with believing hearts what measureless grace and goodness Christ hath shown to us, in that for us He offered up to His Father His life and blood upon the Cross. After this exhortation, he reads the Gospel concerning the Lord's Supper, as the three Evangelists and Paul in I Corinthians xi have described it. Then the minister distributes the Bread and the Cup of the Lord among them, having partaken of them also himself. The congregation then sing again a hymn of praise; and afterwards the minister closes the Supper with a short prayer, blesses the people, and lets them go in the peace of the Lord. This is the manner and custom with which we now celebrate the Lord's Supper on Sundays only.[5]

The above description does not represent the rite as finally revised. For example, the Epistle and the exhortation upon it were eliminated. The importance of the Strasbourg rite lies primarily in its influence upon Calvin and the Reformation that stemmed from Geneva. It is here that " there emerges, for the first time after the Reformation, the service that was to become the norm of Sunday Morning Worship in the Reformed Churches, namely, the eucharistic service with the offertory, consecration, and communion omitted." [6] Although, as has been mentioned, the practice in Strasbourg cathedral was weekly observance of the Lord's Supper, the procedure of following the general Strasbourg pattern without the Sacrament was to become dominant practice in the Reformed churches of Europe and Scotland.

Bucer had begun his work as a follower of Zwingli. His appreciation of the meaning of worship in the life of the Christian community led him away from the stark simplicity of the Zurich Reformer to a richer and more traditional liturgy. His influence was to have great impact upon the Calvinist tradition through John Calvin himself. Bucer combined a strong sense of Biblical authority with a vigorous appreciation for the doctrine of the Holy Spirit. Nothing is to be done that cannot be interpreted as true to " the clear and plain declarations" of the Bible. No external forms are to be relied upon to seal the word of God to the human heart. This is the work of the Holy Spirit. Preaching was central in the Strasbourg rites. There were to be three sermons a day and they were to be arranged so that a person might surely be able to attend two of them. The first service was in the morning, " after five o'clock in winter and about four in summer." The second service was at 8 A.M. each day, summer and winter, and the third was an evening service at 4 P.M. in summer and at 3 in the winter. Although Luther had restored preaching to a central place in the worship experience of the church, it was left to the Zwingli-Bucer-Calvin school to exalt it to preeminence.

From 1538 to 1541 Calvin was minister to a congregation of French exiles in Strasbourg. This was during the time of Calvin's own exile from Geneva and in a period of his life when he was wrestling with his own views of the Eucharist, which had been unacceptable to Geneva. In his ministry to the Strasbourg group Calvin adopted almost word for word the Strasbourg liturgy and published his own service book in French based upon it. When he was recalled to Geneva, he took with him the Strasbourg rite, adapted it to his situation and views in minor ways, but retained its essential structure. He reduced the number of variants in the prayers and added what Maxwell describes as " a long and tiresome paraphrase of the Lord's Prayer." [7] In accordance with his theological emphasis upon the importance of obedience to God's law he introduced a metrical version of the Decalogue with a collect for God's grace to keep us in obedience, thus separating the two Tables of the Law. He also included the use of the Nunc Dimittis after the Eucharist. Beyond these his changes were minor and in wording only. " If the Strasbourg rite was derived from the Mass," comments Bard Thompson, " Calvin preferred not to stare at that misfortune, but rather to believe that the work of Schwarz and Bucer conformed to the practice of the primitive church." [8]

The Genevan service of 1542 for Sunday morning worship went somewhat as follows:

Our help is in the name of the Lord, who made heaven and
    earth. Amen.
Confession of Sin
Words of absolution or assurance
Psalm sung by the Congregation
Prayer for Illumination by minister
Collect for Illumination
Scripture Lesson
Sermon
Prayers of Intercession and Supplication
(When the Lord's Supper is celebrated a prayer of prepara-
    tion is joined to the above prayers and the service pro-
    ceeds as follows:)
Words of Institution and Exhortation
Distribution of Elements (The people were to come forward
    as Psalms were sung or a portion of Scripture read)
Thanksgiving after the Supper
Song of Simeon — *Nunc Dimittis*
Benediction [9]

Calvin carried on a long warfare with the Genevan church authorities as to the frequency of the celebration of Communion. His insistence upon a weekly observance was unavailing, and, although his opinion never changed, in practice he was forced to occasional celebration. As a result the view held by all the major Reformers except Zwingli that the twofold ministry of grace by means of Word and Sacrament should be restored to the church was lost. Whereas the medieval church had lost sight of the importance of the Word due to the degeneration of preaching, the Protestants were to lose sight of the Eucharist. In consequence the idea is held by many Protestants today that the Reformers deliberately set out to replace the Mass with the sermon. Nothing was farther from the thought of John Calvin. He maintained the importance of both Word and Sacrament as the " means of grace." His view of the nature of the Sacrament of the Lord's Supper was not as extreme as Zwingli's nor as close to transubstantiation as Luther's.

He affirmed the Real Presence as did Luther and asserted that the bread and wine were more than symbols. He attempted to strike a middle way between Luther and Zwingli. Although agreeing with Zwingli in denying that the Communion was a sacrifice, he was unwilling to go as far as Zwingli in stressing the memorial significance of the feast. " His own somewhat subtle theory," observed C. J. Cadoux, " was that the reality of the participation in the body and blood was guaranteed, not by their physical or corporeal presence, but by their dynamic effect on the soul of the participant." [10]

It is extremely difficult to delineate the varying views of the Lord's Supper as held by the major Reformers, for they shade into one another. Zwingli plainly stressed the fact that the body of Christ was in heaven at the right hand of God and not in the bread and wine in any but a symbolic sense. Luther affirmed a more realistic and immediate presence of Christ in the bread and wine but was careful to avoid identification of the Presence with the elements. Calvin more directly related the Presence with the receptivity of the believer. These views are largely matters of emphasis, but the consequences were to prove serious.

The door to an ultimate subjectivity in worship as opposed to the ultimate objectivity of the Mass of the Middle Ages was to be pushed farther and farther open. Yet Calvin himself did not conceive of the influence of the Eucharist solely in terms of its impact upon the participants. He attempted to retain a vital sense of the Real Presence apart from the feelings of the worshipers. Donald Baillie, writing of Calvin's attempts in this area of theological thought, says: " He speaks in the most literal way of the flesh of Christ being present in the sacrament. He has to reconcile this with the body of Christ being actually in heaven, at an immense distance from the earth, and to him it is simply a mystery and a miracle that through the supernatural power of God this distance is bridged and the flesh of Christ is present. Of course he does not teach that the body and blood of Christ are locally present *in the elements;* yet they are spiritually present – not merely believed or imagined to be present, but truly and really present to the faith of the believer. Obviously Calvin is trying very hard to secure the utmost objectivity and reality for the presence of Christ in the sacrament, and at the same time to avoid all the magical, mechanical, and spatial implications of saying that the body and blood of Christ are *in* the bread and the wine, or that there is a change in the elements such as is defined by the Roman doctrine of transubstantiation." [11]

On the whole, Calvin's impulse was to move farther from the Roman pattern of worship than Luther had done. Whereas Luther assumed that what was not forbidden by Scripture was allowable, Calvin's approach began from a reverse principle – whatever is not taught in Scripture is not allowable. This was essentially Bucer's position in Strasbourg. In Calvin's practice this principle was behind much of the sweeping aside of the ceremonialism of the medieval church. At the same time he retained dignity and order, a carefully structured pattern of worship, and a sense of the wholeness of worship that Zwingli lacked in his excessive rationalism. His effort to keep the Eucharist along with the preached Word at the center of worship indicates his sense of the importance of the acted drama of the redemptive act of God in Christ. The way in which Calvin employed his principle of bringing to bear upon worship practices the judgment of Scripture may be illustrated in his attitude toward kneeling in prayer.

I approve of no human constitutions, except such as are founded on the authority of God, and deduced from the Scripture, so that they may be considered as altogether Divine. Let us take, as an example, the kneeling practised during solemn prayers. The question is, whether it be a human tradition, which every one is at liberty to reject or neglect. I answer that it is at once both human and Divine. It is of God, as it forms a branch of that decorum which is recommended to our attention and observance by the apostle; it is of men, as it particularly designates that which had in general been rather hinted than clearly expressed. From this single example, it is easy to judge what opinion ought to be entertained of all the rest. . . . In external discipline and ceremonies, he has not been pleased to give us minute directions what we ought to do in every particular case, forseeing that this would depend on the different circumstances of different periods, and knowing that one form would not be adapted to all ages, — here we must have recourse to the general rules which he has given, that to them may be conformed all the regulations which shall be necessary to the decorum and order of the Church. . . . As he has delivered no express injunctions on this subject, because these things are not necessary to salvation, and ought to be applied to the edification of the Church, with a variety suitable to the manners of each age and nation, therefore, as the benefit of the Church shall require, it will be right to change and abolish former regulations, and to institute new ones. . . . We ought not to resort to innovation rashly or frequently, or for trivial causes.[12]

In short, Calvin's principle of following Scripture and basing worship procedure on its teaching was not the kind of rigid, unimaginative literalism some later Calvinists displayed. Such a phrase as " decorum and order " was to be interpreted in the light of good sense and in the light of the cultural situation in which the church ministered. In the matter of kneeling, Calvin came down squarely on the side of this posture as most acceptable. In the same spirit of " decorum and order " he rejected the idea of extempore prayer and in his liturgy all the prayers were fixed, to be read by the minister. Although discarding the elaborate garments of the priest of the Roman Church, he retained the simple cassock and academic gown as suitable garb for the clergy. He felt that the significance of the festivals and emphases of the church year should not be lost. In the name of Calvin subsequent generations were to display what to him would have been shocking violations of " decorum and order." Calvin, although not as medieval in his orientation as Luther, held the traditions of the church, where they did not obviously contradict Scriptural admonitions or doctrine, in high regard. The bareness and ugliness of which Calvinism has been accused in its worship were not characteristic of the Genevan Reformer but of his less imaginative successors in the seventeenth and eighteenth centuries. Simplicity was his aim, and the unnecessary bric-a-brac of ornamentation were an abhorrance to him. This did not mean, however, that he descended to the banality that has been attributed to him. This was reserved for later generations.

CHAPTER 8

The Word Among the Scots and the English

The influence of the Lutheran Reformation in worship was not extensive beyond Germany and the Scandinavian countries. The influence of Calvin, modified to a large extent by Zwingli as the more radical groups such as the Puritans became powerful, was to become the norm in France, southern Germany, Holland, Denmark, and Scotland, as well as in Switzerland. There were variations in all of these lands but the basic hallmark of simplicity and the principle that Scriptural authority should be observed in the realm of worship characterized Protestantism wherever Calvin's influence obtained. In Scotland the influence of the English Reformation determined worship practices at first. The Anglican Prayer Book of 1552 was in general use. The prayer book of 1549 had been largely the work of Thomas Cranmer. He had taken most of his material from Roman service books and in the service of Communion had preserved the essential movements of the Roman Mass. However, he had translated the Latin into English that was characterized by an incomparable literary style and beauty, perfectly suited to a liturgy. "Cranmer's work," says T. S. Garrett, "must take its place as a literary classic alongside the King James Version of the Bible and the plays of Shakespeare which belong to the same golden age of English literature."[1] When Cranmer's liturgy of 1549 was revised in a more Protestant direction in 1552, most of the language of the original work was retained. It forms the continuing basis for the Episcopal Book of Common Prayer which maintains into the present an incomparable influence upon liturgical expression.

The modifications of 1552 were in part due to the violent pronouncements of John Knox, who, acting as a royal chaplain at the court of King Edward VI, had attacked the custom of kneeling to receive the Sacrament of the Lord's Supper. What came to be called " The Black Rubric " was inserted, declaring that although kneeling was required for the sake of reverence and humility, it by no means implied adoration of the elements themselves, which were not changed from their natural substance by the act of consecration. Some rearrangement of prayers took place and changes in order of progression. The Decalogue was inserted. The most important change was the omission of the Epiklesis or prayer for the blessing of the Holy Spirit, and the elimination of the Anamnesis or the words of remembrance of Christ. Participation by the congregation in the elements in both kinds was allowed, and the use of the vernacular was required. The words of the celebrant were to be audible. At the same time more of the flavor of the Latin Mass was retained than in any other Protestant liturgy. Dom Gregory Dix strongly insists that the revisions of 1552 reflect a Zwinglian theology of the Eucharist on the part of Cranmer, asserting that the rearrangement of the prayers enabled them to serve " with remarkably few changes to express the full Zwinglian doctrine." [2] Though Cranmer may have been greatly influenced by Zwingli's individualistic concept of memorialism, it is hard to see the revisions of 1552 as a deliberate attempt to force the Communion into Zwingli's theological framework. Instead, it appears to have been a compromise effort to preserve as much of the old structure as possible in the face of a more radical Protestantism. As such it succeeded for a time. Designated as a Communion, not a Mass, it was intended to be celebrated at least weekly. Both the nature of the service and the frequency of its observance were thoroughly acceptable to the churches of England and the churches of Scotland. John Knox said he could " think well of it." However, upon the accession of Mary Tudor to the English throne in 1553 and the revival of Roman Catholic persecution, Knox with others of the Protestant faith fled to the Continent.

For the next five years Knox spent most of his time in Geneva at the feet of John Calvin. When he returned to his native land upon invitation in 1559, he brought with him an unyielding admiration for the Calvinist movement and an unchanging commitment to its principles of reformation, not only in the field of theology but of worship as well. According to Bard Thompson, " he noted certain ' diabolical inventions' in the Prayer Book and pronounced Anglican worship a ' mingle-mangle.' " [3] Even though Mary Tudor was dead and the Protestant Queen Elizabeth was on the throne of England, Knox launched into an attack on the ceremonies that he considered popish which were still a part of the ritual of the church. He introduced his Service Book, which he had prepared for the use of the English congregation in Geneva and which was based largely on the Form of Prayers from Calvin's own Service Book. The Knox liturgy did not supercede completely the revised Prayer Book of 1552 in Scotland, but its influence increased as the Church of England under Elizabeth adopted a further revision in 1559 that was generally used in England. This was The Book of Common Prayer which remained the service book of the Church of England until 1662 when the final revisions were made which have obtained unto the present.

Knox's service, being closely dependent upon that of Calvin, was marked by the same simplicity of design. It began with a Confession of Sins and a Prayer for Pardon, followed by a Psalm. Prayer for Illumination preceded the reading of the Scripture and the sermon. The Prayers of Intercession, the Lord's Prayer, the affirmation of the Creed, the singing of a Psalm, and the Benediction followed. The plainness of this service is evident. According to Knox's Genevan order, the Lord's Supper was to be commonly observed once a month or " so oft as the congregation shall think expedient." However, by the time Knox had returned to Scotland he was able to say, " Four times in the year we think sufficient to the administration of the Lord's Table, which we desire to be distincted, that the superstition of times may be avoided so far as may be." [4] The elements were to be received by the people sitting, not in their pews but at tables in the nave as they came forward in groups. The manner of administration required:

The Words of Institution
Exhortation
Prayer of Thanksgiving
Fraction
Delivery to the people, who take the bread which the minister has broken and distribute and divide it among themselves, likewise passing the cup. Appropriate Scripture is to be read by the minister during the Delivery.
Prayer of Thanksgiving
Psalm 103 (or some other Psalm of thanks)
Blessing [5]

The interplay between the worship life of Scotland and England was important to the liturgies of the churches of both nations. It is necessary to recognize that the difference did not grow to the intensity that came to be felt solely on the grounds of theological divergencies. They were not problems of the church solely as a church. The religious life of each nation was deeply entwined with its political life. It is difficult to judge as we look back whether John Knox was more important in the life of Scotland as a politician or as a churchman. Certainly his influence remained in both aspects of Scottish history long after his death. " Of all the Reformations," writes Will Durant, " the Scottish shed the least blood and was the most permanent." [6] It was definitely permanent in its sense of separation from the Church of England in the seventeenth century.

James VI of Scotland who became James I of England in 1603 hoped that the Scots with their *Forme of Prayers* or Book of Common Order which Knox had brought into use in 1560 might be induced to move closer to the English Book of Common Prayer in order that the two peoples might share a uniform liturgy. The Scots clung without budging to their *Forme of Prayers*. They rejected James's efforts to interfere in the life of the church with violence and without qualification. Charles I in 1637 attempted by force to do what his father had attempted less dramatically. On the authority of the crown he issued a directive that henceforth Archbishop Laud's revision of The Book of Common Prayer should be the liturgy for the Scottish Church. Charles's major initial error lay in his failure to consult the leaders in Scotland. Behind the scenes there lay the smoldering resentment of the Scots against Charles's appointments and various attempts to interfere in church life. Behind this was the whole history of English-Scottish conflict of more than a century. Independence for the Scots involved the independence of their church. It may be said that the struggle for Scottish freedom revolved around the struggle for the freedom of the church from English dominance.

Charles had married a Roman Catholic, to the consternation of the Scots. Then he had extended the authority of the English bishops over the Scottish presbyteries. He had placed five bishops and one archbishop upon the Privy Council of Scotland. Along with these high-handed acts that so alarmed the Presbyterians, he had incensed the nobility by revoking all grants of church or crown lands that had been made since the reign of Mary Stuart. Scotland was seething with turmoil and resentment. It was against this turbulent background that Charles had come north to be crowned in 1633. The ritual that accompanied his coronation was an Anglican rite complete with candles and altar, vestments and crucifix. The liturgical rules that the bishops drew up for the Scots " gave the king full jurisdiction over all ecclesiastical matters, forbade assemblies of the clergy except at the king's call, restricted the right of teaching to persons licensed by a bishop, and limited ordination to candidates accepting these canons. Charles sanctioned the canons and ordered them proclaimed in all Scottish churches." [7] Efforts to enforce the canons intensified the conflict. It was in protest against the ritual that a riot broke out in St. Giles church in Edinburgh when Jenny Geddes flung her famous stool at the officiating dean with the words, " Thou foul thief, wilt thou say Mass at my lug [ear]? "

We cannot help wondering how far the rejection of the liturgy of the church was an expression of a deeper rejection of anything English and especially of anything promulgated by King Charles. The signing of the National Covenant in 1638 and then of the Solemn League and Covenant in 1643, which gave the designation " Covenanters " to Scottish history and legend, were semipolitical and semi-ecclesiastical reactions. Bishops were deposed, and Presbyterianism became more than a form of Christian faith. It became a national passion. Open warfare broke out, and the Scots embraced their nationalistic aspirations and their Presbyterian independence with equal zeal. *The Forme of Prayers* and The Book of Common Order were restored as the sources of the liturgy and worship. Charles found himself in trouble in England and his energies were diverted from Scotland. Presbyterianism settled itself in positions of authority in the church, and Anglicanism, both as to polity and form of worship, was rejected. Unfortunately, some congregations, having rejected Charles's attempt to enforce use of The Book of Common Prayer, did not return to Knox's liturgy but attempted innovations. A new influence had invaded Scotland from the south. It was the influence of the English Puritans.

The Puritans had been growing in power for some time.

As Dr. Durant points out, there were so many parties among them that it is a rare generalization that can hold of them all. In worship, however, some generalizations can be made. They were addicted to a concept of worship that was " unceremonious, legalitarian, and divorced from the distractions of religious art. . . . To most Puritans music, stained glass, religious images, surplices, anointed priests were obstacles to direct communion with God. . . . As Protestantism had stressed the sermon beyond Catholic precedent, so Puritanism expanded it even beyond Protestant custom. A hunger for sermons gnawed at some hearts; the mayor of Norwich moved to London to hear more preaching; a mercer resigned from a congregation because it provided only one sermon per Sunday. Special ' lecturers ' arose to ease this hunger — laymen hired by a parish to preach a Sunday sermon additional to what the regular minister offered." [8] The Puritans traced much of their theology and their sturdy ethical emphases to Calvin and Geneva. But they moved far from Calvin in their attitude toward the liturgy and in their worship practices. As a matter of fact, Zwingli's influence was more important than that of Calvin. His rationalism, his subjectivism, his rejection of the arts and of symbols, far more extreme than were Calvin's, were the characteristics that the Puritans displayed and developed. They emphasized worship as a matter of the inner spirit. It is from them that the custom of extempore prayer stems.

Strangely enough for such a democratic movement, the effect of much of their procedure was to take away much of the congregational participation that the Reformation had restored. Responses and litanies, congregational collects and general prayers, were abolished in favor of free prayer by the minister. It was felt that he, under the inspiration of the Holy Spirit, could phrase utterances expressive of the needs and wants of the people in a way that no set written forms of prayer could do. One party among them, the Barrowists, went so far in their refusal of any set forms as to eschew even metrical versions of the psalms, singing them from the Bible without regard to time or tune. In every area of worship the Puritans pursued austerity. Their churches were stripped bare of all symbols. They abolished all feasts and special days. They even removed funerals and weddings from the corporate activities of the church. Baird cites the following articles or statements of errors requiring redress in the Anglican Church, drawn up by some of the early nonconformists:

No sacrament ought to be administered without being preceded by a sermon, *preached and not read.*
Sermons ought not to be preached at the burial of the dead.
The Holy Scriptures ought not to be read in the churches.
No one ought to be confined to set forms of prayers.[9]

Puritanism carried to the extreme two forces, individualism and subjectivity. Both these forces had begun to manifest themselves in the late Middle Ages. The concept of the church at worship as a corporate reality was lost. The Puritan meetinghouse held a collection of individuals at prayer. The meaning of the service lay in what happened within the individual. Quite logically, some Puritan groups rejected infant baptism because it was evident that the child was not capable of undergoing an " experience." The central place of the sermon created a reliance upon the verbal communication of the faith that obviated other types of symbol. In the realm of moral quality Puritan life was admirable, although stern and even trivial at times. " They carried morality to excess, as later ages carried liberty," says Durant, " but perhaps their inhuman code was a necessary corrective to the loose morals of Elizabethan England. . . . To them, in part, England owes the solid sobriety of the British character, the stability of the British family, and the integrity of Britain's official life." [10] No comparable tribute can be paid to their influence upon Protestant worship. Although it can be understood that much of their procedure was reaction against the inertia of the English church regarding reformation, the fact remains that so much was lost in the Puritan reaction that Protestantism today, especially in America, suffers from their influence.

Ilion T. Jones, who is wary of liturgies and decries the current trend in the American church in his *A Historical Approach to Evangelical Worship*, attributes two purposes to the English Puritans — " namely, to restore English worship to the purity, spirituality, and simplicity of the New Testament church, and to rid that worship of its Roman characteristics, or ' papal errors ' as they were usually called." However, Jones goes on to declare, with great understatement:

In a number of ways they went beyond the Calvinistic reformers on the Continent. Calvin approved of a set form of prayers, of the festivals of the Christian year, of the pronouncement of absolution by the ministers, of confirmation, of communion to the sick, of auricular confession, of weekly communion, of funerals and marriages as ecclesiastical activities, and of the use of vestments. He permitted the use of the signing of the cross in baptism, of the ring in marriage, and kneeling while receiving the elements, three ceremonies the Puritans opposed as superstitions. In many instances the Separatists such as the Barrowists, the Brownists, and the Anabaptists went even further than the moderate Puritans. They opposed all liturgical forms.[11]

This was the influence that was now to have consequences of such great moment in the worship of the Scottish Church and, less directly, upon the worship of the Reformed churches on the Continent. The opposition to symbols and liturgical forms was significant. The deeper psychological orientation of worship in the direction of individualism and subjectivity was even more significant. The central meaning of corporate worship as an act of the church was being changed. In the Middle Ages this meaning was obscured by the centralization of the act of worship upon an altar presided over by priests with a congregation of spectators. In the Puritan movement the meaning was fragmented into acts of worship engaged in by a collection of Christians who gathered together bound by the fellowship of a common creed. The full implications of the Puritan movement were only to be recognized in the life of the American denominations in the nineteenth century.

CHAPTER 9

The Word Among the Puritans

The Reformation on the Continent was complete as far as any major developments were concerned. The gains in Christian worship were immense. Once again the congregation participated actively in the services in the singing of hymns, and in general responses and litanies. The vernacular replaced the Latin Mass. Protestants in general rejected the idea of the Eucharist as an objective sacrifice, and the altars once more became tables. S. A. Devan calls this the "greatest of all gains" of the Reformation.[1] The restoration of preaching to a place of centrality may be seen as an equally vital result. Word and Sacrament stood together in the thought of the great Reformers.

On the other hand, the worship life of the church was affected adversely by the fact that with abandonment of the Eucharist as an objective sacrifice went displacement of Communion as the supreme act of Christian worship. Devan calls this the "most important"[2] loss of the Reformation. Alongside this loss must go the Protestant depreciation of art and the consequent loss of symbols. The abuses of the medieval church had made the Reformers suspicious of the lush opulence afforded by the arts in their appeal to the senses. The rich liturgy of the Middle Ages was stripped away, and the simplicity of Christian worship revealed anew. However, the simplicity was prone to degenerate into barrenness. The failure of subsequent generations of reformers, of lesser magnitude than such men as Luther and Calvin, to appreciate the importance of the appeal to the whole of man led to a rejection of those means of communication that are contained in the arts and in symbols. Nowhere was this danger more prevalent than in the Reformed tradition. The Lutheran Church had continued in the tradition of its great leader and retained much of the tradition of the past. The Anglican Church had floundered through a period of compromise and hesitation, complicated by political pressures, to the point where it embraced a wide variation ranging from Roman practices to Protestant procedures influenced by the Puritans *but* always within the framework of the traditional structure of the liturgy of the past.

In Scotland, now the most vigorous center of the Calvinistic influence, the political and social conflicts had tremendous repercussions on the patterns of worship. The violent and emotional rejection of the English liturgy combined with a feeling of kinship for the dissenting English Puritans led the Scots to embrace Puritan principles and practices. Following the downfall of King Charles, the English Parliament commissioned an assembly of divines to meet in Westminster Abbey and evolve a plan of church government, a confession of faith, and a form of worship. Scottish representatives who were present as nonvoting participants, exercised great influence upon the work of the assembly, and the ensuing Westminster Confession of Faith was to become a historic document of Presbyterianism in Scotland and America. The Directory of Public Worship which the Assembly produced was also accepted by the Scottish Assembly in 1645 along with a Form of Presbyterial Government. None of these documents had enduring influence in England, except among Presbyterians, but they were vital to the future of the Church of Scotland. The Directory for Public Worship showed the influence of Knox's *The Forme of Prayers* as well as of The Book of Common Prayer, and retained the general structure of the liturgy that had been common to Christianity for centuries. The Scottish suspicion of the Church of England's influence surrounded it nonetheless, and the practices of the English Puritans were widespread. The result was disuse of the Directory to the extent that the traditional pattern was drastically changed in the direction of an exaggerated freedom from form. There was as a consequence a " decline in the due ordering of public worship which followed the Cromwellian period, and which lasted until the mid-nineteenth century." [3]

In the observance of the Lord's Supper the decline was precipitate. The difficulty in securing an ordained minister as celebrant led to increasingly infrequent observances of the Supper. While The Book of Common Order recommended monthly Communion and the Westminster Directory stated that " communion is frequently to be celebrated," the practice of the Scots became one of infrequent parish observance. During the early seventeenth century, Communion was rarely celebrated more than once a year in most parishes. It must be added, however, that the practice arose of several parishes joining together and closing their churches except for the church in the parish in which the Sacrament was being celebrated. In this way, by traveling to a neighboring parish most Scots could participate in the Communion several times a year. Great solemnity and reverence attended the services. They often made great impact upon the worshipers. In the long run, however, there was a gradual decline in attendance and appeal, with the occasional parish observance becoming the only sacramental experience most Scots attended. The failure to make the Eucharist central to parish worship led to a decline in its significance for church life.

It was not alone the parish celebration of frequent Communion that was lost. As Howard Hageman writes: " By the close of the seventeenth century the liturgy had entirely ceased to be a living thing in the Scottish Kirk. The coveted freedom of Puritanism became the established order." [4] The Puritans objected to the reading of the Scriptures at public worship unless they were expounded as they were read. While few if any churches went so far as not to read Scripture at all, there were ministers who read brief excerpts and who replaced the lectionary with " lecturing " upon Scripture. The use of the Lord's Prayer, the Doxology, and the metrical psalms declined as smacking of episcopacy. The Apostles' Creed fell under the same shadow. Extempore prayers, long and tedious, became the fashion. The posture of the congregation at prayer, kneeling being frowned upon, became careless, many sitting and some standing. After a time standing became general. Vestments were discarded for nearly a century. The Christian year fell into the discard, to be replaced by a rigid Puritan Sabbatarianism. No wonder Miss Evelyn Underhill can write with justice:

Under the influence of a Puritanism introduced from England and superimposed on Calvinism, liturgical quality was gradually lost, preaching more and more vanquished worship; and in the bad years of the eighteenth century, the services had declined to a level of uncouthness and even irreverence which a sympathetic historian can describe as " unparalleled in Christendom." [5]

Quite frequently one hears an American Presbyterian say in protest against liturgy, symbols, or vestments: " I'm a good Scotch Presbyterian. I just cannot accept such things." Actually this was not " good Scotch Presbyterianism." It would have horrified Calvin and spurred John Knox to righteous wrath. The extremes of free worship that have characterized American Presbyterianism were expressions of English Puritanism embraced by Scotch Presbyterians in a chaotic period of national life when anti-English emotions centered in a rejection of anything shared with the Anglican Church. A restoration of the true heritage of the Scotch Presbyterian Church was not to come until the latter part of the nineteenth century. In the meanwhile American Presbyterianism had been indelibly stamped with the public services of the eighteenth-century Church of Scotland which, says Principal Story, " had become probably the baldest and rudest in Christendom." [6]

It must be stressed that worship throughout Christendom, although not as " bald and rude " as in Scotland, was at low ebb. This is true of the Lutherans and Anglicans as well as of the Reformed churches on the Continent. The Continental version of Puritanism was Pietism. Liturgical integrity was lost and, says Hageman, of the Dutch church, " By the mid-eighteenth century free prayer had become not only the accepted rule but the standard by which the ability and religious zeal of the ministry were judged. If a minister could not pray freely and movingly for at least half an hour, he was clearly not right with God." Dr. Hageman sums up the situation at the beginning of the nineteenth century by saying:

In Great Briton, the Netherlands, much of Germany, and the United States, the liturgy had almost entirely disappeared. . . . Kneeling or standing for prayer and standing for praise, once good Reformed customs, had been replaced by sitting for everything. The Christian year had almost entirely disappeared. The Eucharist was so infrequent as to be negligible. The one significant element in a service, symbolized by the one imposing piece of furniture in the church, was the sermon. . . . The impartial observer surveying the liturgical life of the Reformed churches in, let us say, 1820 could have justifiably concluded that it was just about finished.[7]

It is instructive that the decline in the worship of Protestantism paralleled a decline in the spread of its influence in other areas. Following the great initial impact of the Reformation and the ensuing decades of energetic expansion, Roman Catholicism renewed its vigor and the Protestant movement slowed down to a desperate staying action in much of Europe. Furthermore, its spiritual vitality was weak and its ethical impact feeble. This was generally true of all branches of the movement stemming from the Reformation. In Kenneth Scott Latourette's carefully schematized story of Christianity in terms of advance and recession he points to 1750 as marking what seemed to be another major recession in the Christian tide.[8] Is it not possible that the "bald and rude" worship procedures of so much of the Protestant Church have a bearing upon this lack of vitality? The question of priority may be debatable but the fact of regression and of concurrent loss of worship vitality is clear. The impact of the new missionary movement breathed new life into the church and what appeared to be a "major recession" proved to be the prelude to a great advance. The historical reality of this new factor does not answer the question, however, as to how far the loss of effective worship symbols may have caused Protestantism to be bereft of real communication with the newly emerging industrial society to which it attempted to minister. Worship must keep in touch with the unchanging with a due recognition of the changed. The practices of Protestantism certainly reflect the new age at many points. Worship was democratized to a great degree. The doctrine of the priesthood of all believers was distorted into a doctrine of every man his own priest, an idea that would have puzzled Luther. Individualism was given large rein and the sense of community the Middle Ages had known tumbled before it. Protestantism reflected this change. The church as a corporate entity, different in a sense from and more than the individual members of the congregation, was lost. Believer's baptism was practiced by an ever-enlarging segment of the church.

While Protestantism was reflecting the new values of a new epoch of history, some good and some bad, she was not always wedding the contemporary with the unchanging realities of her faith in creative ways. For example, the sacramentarian view of the Middle Ages was crassly unscientific and incredibly out of tune with the newly emerging scientific mind. The response of the Protestant movement to this fact was not a reinterpretation of the Eucharist but a practical abandonment of it. This was true even of the Church of England which had in theory retained the Communion as its central act of worship. In practice the

Anglicans had lost their high view of the Sacrament. Celebration in the seventeenth and eighteenth centuries was less frequent and less stressed in the Established Church than in the Free Churches. The sermons were heavily laden with the rationalistic moralism of the Enlightenment. Horton Davies cites the " sheer worldliness of so many of the official representatives of the church " as an even more serious delinquency. " The perfunctory tones of the clergyman, who might be wearing his hunting clothes and spurs beneath his cassock and Genevan gown as he raced through the service in his eagerness to get to the social diversions of the day, seemed often to reduce the liturgy to mere play-acting, in which the fashionable members of the auditory acquiesced." [9] The decline of vital worship in the Anglican communion was to reach its nadir in the nineteenth century. On Easter Day in 1800, for example, at St. Paul's Cathedral in London only six communicants were present for the single celebration of the Lord's Supper the cathedral afforded.

Again, the new age was one in which the reason, the intellect, conceptual thought, and consequent verbalization were all dominant aspects of man's approach to the universe. Protestantism with intuitive appreciation of this fact made use of reasoned theological formula, of the sermon, and of other symbols, including hymns, which were essentially verbal in character and capable of conveying the kind of meanings apt to appeal most to the new " modern man." At the same time, ageless means of communication of truth fell into desuetude — the arts and nonverbal symbols. As a result the church failed in its worship to meet the whole man. It came to rely upon preaching to a far greater degree than was warranted by a historical appreciation of the meaning of worship. It was absolutely essential that the preached Word regain its place alongside the Eucharist in Christian worship. In view of the denigration of preaching in the Middle Ages the Reformer's emphasis upon its restoration was not only understandable but necessary. In Calvin's Geneva *aller au sermon* meant " to go to church " and

Calvin himself spoke of attendance upon public worship as *fréquenter les sermons*. This emphasis was not intended to obliterate the church's liturgy nor its Sacraments. It in fact did come almost to obliterate them, and the fuzzy knowledge of the history of worship led Protestantism to the verge of futility in the late seventeenth and eighteenth centuries.

In the meanwhile, a whole new continent was opened and it proved to be largely a Protestant continent. The Spanish and the French colonization of what was to become the United States was episodic and passing in influence. The British, with some aid from the Dutch, and the Swedes, colonized that portion of the North American continent which was to become a great Protestant nation until the middle of the twentieth century. The predominant influence in the religious life of the colonies was Puritan. With the Puritan theology and ethic we are not directly concerned, although worship practices cannot be dissociated from either. It is with the expression of Puritanism in the worship life of the American church that we will be concerned, for the contemporary liturgical revival cannot be seen for what it is apart from this background. Although the Church of England was the established church of Virginia and New York, the Puritan influence in even this staunchly liturgical church was evident. As far as the rest of the colonies were concerned the Protestantism that flourished was predominantly Calvinist in theology and Puritan in ethic and worship. Of the Congregationalists in New England, George Stephenson writes:

The Puritan churches were preaching and teaching churches. The services were educational. The emphasis was on the sermon. In New England labor and intelligence went hand in hand and so did religion and intelligence. The faithful assembled in the meetinghouse to pray and to meditate, to sing psalms, and to hear the Scripture read and expounded by a learned man. Once a month the Lord's Supper was celebrated — not as a sacrament but as memorial observance. In reality, the faithful met for edification, rather than for worship.[10]

The prayers were long and exhortatory. The sermons were longer and didactic. The setting was often bare, completely devoid of any appeal to the sensuous. Since, for a time, the New England Puritan worship was an authentic expression of a theological position in which stress was laid upon the law against a background of the transcendence of God, reality was communicated and the service was meaningful. An architecture was created, expressive of the finest values of Puritan society, and the New England meetinghouse still has no serious rival as an authentic artistic product of an indigenous faith. Its pulpit-centered design reflected the centrality of the sermon and the Bible. Its clear windows symbolized the letting in of the light of God's Word upon the worshipers. Its simplicity represented the directness of the Puritan faith in a creed and a moral law. The very name " meetinghouse " implied the called of the Lord who came together to hear the Word read and expounded.

Such a type of worship could not appeal to the whole man. There was an absence of color, ceremony, sensuousness. How far did this affect subsequent generations to whom the immediacy of the Puritan experience was not vital? In the meanwhile, however, the general pattern of Puritan worship had so influenced American Christianity that it had become the norm for all save those churches, such as the Lutheran and the Anglican, historically committed to a more traditional liturgy. Other influences were operative, including the cultural setting of American society, the burgeoning frontier with its lack of ordained clergy, and the psychology of an individualistic young nation accustomed to look with jaundiced eyes upon the traditions and customs of the Continent that had been left behind. The factors leading to the rejection of the liturgical heritage of the church in Scotland and among some groups in Europe were intensified as they found expression in American life.

CHAPTER 10

The Word on the American Frontier

Following the successful War for Independence by the American colonies, there were two denominations that were in a commanding position in American society. One was the Congregationalist and the other was the Presbyterian. Both were Calvinistic in theology and Puritan in worship. The tradition of the Congregationalist was English. The tradition of the Presbyterian was Scotch, but it was the Scotland of Cromwell's day, and the practices of the American Presbyterians at their worship were far removed from those of Geneva or of Knox's Edinburgh. The Baptists were active in parts of New England, in the western part of Virginia, and in the Carolina back country. True to their heritage of adult baptism and individual experience, their churches were free from anything that smacked of sacerdotalism. Prior to the Revolution the Methodists had grown rather rapidly in some of the colonies, but Wesley's support of the crown during the struggle for freedom had cast a temporary shadow of suspicion over those who were his followers. The Anglican Church was under a deeper shadow made darker and longer by the fact that many of her rectors had been Loyalists. The Lutheran groups were usually isolated into national churches with ties of language and custom to Europe. It can be seen from such a cursory summary that the major influences on the worship life of the church in the new United

States were nonliturgical. When the influence of the Quakers, which was considerable in certain areas, is added, the atmosphere was that in which a free, informal tradition of worship was bound to develop.

The historical situation must be noted. William Warren Sweet points to the bitter struggle in the years just before the American Revolution between the Congregationalists and Presbyterians on one side and the Anglicans on the other over the question of an Anglican bishop for the colonies.

To them [the Congregationalists and the Presbyterians] the presence of an Anglican bishop in America meant nothing less than ecclesiastical tyranny. . . . Writing in 1815, John Adams stated that, " the apprehension of episcopacy contributed, fifty years ago, as much as any other cause, to arouse the attention, not only of the inquiring mind, but of the common people, and urge them to close thinking on the constitutional authority of Parliament over the colonies. . . . This was a fact as certain as any in the history of North America." [1]

It can almost be said that a conflict over church government was a decisive motivating factor in the revolt of the colonies. For in this conflict the Presbyterians and Congregationalists " had become fully convinced," says another church historian, " that religious liberty for them stood or fell with the civil liberties of the colonies. As the tension between London and the colonies increased, the Presbyterians became more vigorous in their support of all organizations and plans for the ' preservation of our liberties.' " [2] The meaning of this for worship becomes plainer if we see, as the colonists unquestionably did, the dreaded Anglican bishop with The Book of Common Prayer in his hand. The majority of Presbyterians in the colonies were from Ulster. These immigrants, usually called Scotch-Irish, were vehement in their hatred of England and scarcely less so in their hatred of the Church of England. The Anglican bishops in the Irish House of Lords had joined in the acts of the Irish Parliament that had not only ruined the Ulstermen economically but had proscribed their clergy from carrying out the functions of ministry.

This rejection of all that smacked of the Church of England extended to the Methodists. Prior to the Revolution the association of the Methodist societies with the Anglican Church had been close. Wesley himself as a loyal Anglican encouraged this relationship. Following the war, the Methodists, already smarting under criticism for Wesley's position, drew away from the somewhat shattered Anglican remnant. Wesley ordained deacons, elders, and superintendents for the American church and prepared a liturgy for their use. This liturgy, prepared for a church that suffered from a lack of ordained priests, was a simple abridgement of The Book of Common Prayer entitled " The Sunday Services for the Methodists of North America, with other Occasional Services." Extempore prayer was allowed and the absolution was turned into a prayer for pardon. Other changes were minor verbal ones. The Methodist Church became a movement of energy and vigor. Its strong emphasis upon lay leadership was a source of its power as it moved forward with the frontier.

Wesley's liturgy became a casualty of the lay participation and the exuberant revivalism of the frontier. The order of service he had prepared was gradually discarded as the Methodists entered into the free worship that began to prevail among the churches most indigenous to the new United States. Among the Congregationalists, the Presbyterians, the Baptists, and the Methodists a progressive rejection of any fixed order of worship took place. All of them were influenced by an anti-English bent that included both bishops and formalism. All of them broke ties with the Old World. At the time the Founding Fathers were meeting in Philadelphia to hammer out a constitution for the United States, the Presbyterians were meeting in the same city to hammer out a constitution for the Presbyterian Church in the United States. The Directory of Worship which was appended was, says Trinterud, " little more than a book of counsel for the clergy." [3] It was vastly inferior to the Directory of the Westminster Assembly. In the first draft, pattern prayers were included but these were eliminated from the revised edition of 1788. The Sacraments were to be celebrated and suggestions as to their celebration were offered, but no set forms were included. Even the marriage ceremony was confined to the vows as far as a set form was concerned. There was no funeral service as such. A section of forms of prayer for home use was also deleted from the final 1788 edition. The insistence on absolutely free prayer reigned supreme.

The Puritan freedom in worship suited the scene in which the churches were set in early America. First of all, members of the clergy were in short supply, particularly on the frontier. As the nation advanced westward the denominations that kept abreast of the march were primarily the Methodists and the Baptists. Observance of the Sacraments was infrequent because of the rarity of ordained men to conduct such observance. The result was a further depreciation of the importance of the Eucharist. As training of the ministry became more erratic and as the ideal of an educated clergy dimmed before a combination of the exigencies of the frontier and a growing suspiciousness on the part of the frontierman of too much " book-larning," the whole orientation of the minister toward his calling shifted. Peter Cartwright asserted that " the great mass of our western people wanted a preacher that could mount a stump, a block, or old log, or stand in the bed of a wagon, and without note or manuscript, quote, expound, and apply the word of God to the hearts and consciences of the people." [4] Cartwright ridiculed the young men sent out by missionary boards in the East, especially those who had studied theology in a seminary.

A Methodist preacher in those days, when he felt that God had called him to preach, instead of hunting up a college or Biblical institute, hunted up a hardy pony of a horse, and some travelling apparatus, and with his library always at hand, namely, Bible, Hymn Book, and Discipline, he started, and with a text that never wore out nor grew stale, he cried, " Behold the Lamb of God, that taketh away the sin of the world." [5]

Such a picture may be exaggerated, but the essential facts are valid. If they had not been, the church could not possibly have kept up with the expansion of the United States. Those denominations such as the Episcopalian and the Lutheran which insisted upon proper training and proper ordination fell behind immediately. The two dominant groups, the Congregationalists and the Presbyterians, after much agonizing and controversy over the degree to which they would compromise in their concept of the ministry in the light of the situation, fell behind gradually at first and then rapidly. The clergyman of the type Peter Cartwright describes was not apt to be meticulous in regard to any kind of ceremony. Church buildings were plain and did not lend themselves to ritual any more than the plain, blunt, direct frontier culture did. Besides, the purpose of the preacher was to preach. Even in his prayers he often preached. He did not have time nor inclination for any liturgy beyond his own primitive one of praying, preaching, and singing.

Related to the concept of the ministry in American life was a concept of salvation. It was individualistic and revivalistic. The purpose of the church was to proclaim " a text that never wore out nor grew stale . . . ' Behold the Lamb of God, that taketh away the sin of the world.' " A church that conceives its task to be one of snatching brands from the burning is not a church that takes worship very seriously aside from those aspects that bear directly upon the conversion of sinners. Preaching was the most effective method of inducing the conversion experience. It was in harmony with the whole individualistic atmosphere of the frontier community. The informal exuberance of the revivalistic preacher was akin to that of the society in which he ministered. Pioneer communities carry few cultural patterns with them and translate them intact to their new environment. They carry even fewer institutional patterns. The emigrants moving westward seldom carried the church. The itinerant preacher, the circuit rider, pursued the westward-bound pioneers zealously and with singular devotion and courage brought Christ to the settlers of the frontier regions. It was not to be expected that they could transplant the church of the ages in its fullness. They did what needed to be done and, humanly speaking, perhaps all that could be done. The aftermath of the rapid westward expansion, however, was a somewhat denuded American church, bereft of much of its heritage of worship and theology. It is no criticism of the frontier preacher to say that he recognized the society to which he ministered, met it on terms that were meaningful and creative, but which were, in the nature of the case, unfinished. The heritage of the frontier still lingers. One peculiar feature of it, which is found again and again in the Ohio Valley, is a feeling that the preacher who does not pray extemporaneously lacks the true credentials a servant of the Lord should hold.

The camp meeting was a frontier institution that provided the major religious experience for multitudes. The spiritual illiteracy of the early eighteenth century was appalling. The camp meeting was school for the religiously illiterate and worship experience for the spiritually destitute. It combined praying, preaching, and singing, all in large and robust doses. Usually there were at least three sermons, an hour or more in length, each day of the meeting. There were long sessions of prayer, and several prayer groups might be going on at the same time. There was much coming and going of people and the feeling of the oneness of a congregation was only come by when the heterogeneous crowd was caught up in an emotional ecstasy through the power of some masterful preacher or the ardor of some frontier hymn.

Peter Cartwright describes a camp meeting near Marietta, Ohio, in 1806, to which the roughs and rowdies of the community as well as the religiously minded came. The toughs came with dirks, clubs, knives, and horsewhips, set to break up the meeting. While Cartwright was preaching on Sunday morning " two well dressed young men marched into the congregation with loaded whips, and hats on, and rose up in the midst of the ladies and began to laugh and talk." After they had responded to a request for order by cursing the preacher, the sermon came to a swift close. Cartwright moved in on the two and precipitated a general free-for-all that ended in the arrest of thirty of the disturbers.[6] Although this is an extreme example of the way the church was forced to operate upon the frontier, it indicates the futility of judgment upon the methods of such men as Peter Cartwright. They spoke the language of their contemporaries and if they failed to confront their constituency with the full impact of the church's message, it is an understandable failure. Nonetheless, we no longer labor under their disabilities and our tendency to cling to the primitivism of a century and a half ago is less understandable.

One other aspect of frontier worship must be mentioned because of its lingering influence. It is frontier singing. Many hymns grew up in the churches of the expanding West. They were in essence folk songs. They reflect several features of frontier religious life. They are buoyant and optimistic and at the same time filled with warnings of death and hell. They are excessively denominational and sectarian. They are subjective and individualistic, moralistic and personal. Dr. Sweet quotes several of them in his *Religion in the Development of American Culture:*

> This day my soul has caught on fire, Hallelujah!
> I feel that heaven is drawing nigher,
>   O glory Hallelujah! . . .
> (Chorus)
> Shout, shout, we're gaining ground, Hallelujah!
> We'll shout old Satan's kingdom down, Hallelujah!

When Christians pray, the Devil runs, Hallelujah!
And leaves the field to Zion's sons,
    O glory Hallelujah!

I long to quit this cumbrous clay, Hallelujah!
And shout with saints in endless day,
    O glory Hallelujah! [7]

The song goes on for nearly twenty other stanzas. An example of the denominational competitiveness is found in the Methodist song that took direct aim at the immersionist groups:

We've searched the law of heaven,
Throughout the Sacred code;
Of Baptism there by dipping
We've never found a word.

To plunge is inconsistant (sic)
Compared with holy rites;
An instance of such business
We've never found as yet. [8]

The Baptists were not to be downed by dogmatic doggerel without replying with some of their own:

Not *at* the River Jordan,
But *in* the flowing stream
Stood John the Baptist preacher
When he baptized Him.

John was a Baptist preacher
When he Baptiz'd the Lamb;
Then Jesus was a Baptist
And thus the Baptist(s) came. [9]

One other example of a frontier hymn shows the all-inclusive nature of Methodist optimism concerning the future of mankind:

The Devil, Calvin and Tom Paine
May hate the Methodists in vain;
Their doctrines shall be downward hurled . . .
The Methodists shall take the world.[10]

Frontier worship was crude and direct. It reflected little sense of tradition and the past. Behind it was a theology of immediacy, " Repent, believe, and be saved." There was little sense of the church, although there was a strong sense of denominational allegiance. It was the individual who counted. The denomination was a collection of like-minded individuals. Worship was less an act of praise and renewal by the church in relation to Almighty God than it was a method of propagandizing for the purpose of converting the unconverted and reassuring the already saved. The sermon, the prayers, the hymns were instruments for edifying the hearers and the participants. The very man-centered nature of his worship was a corollary of his independence and feeling of self-sufficiency.

The one new denomination of significance within the mainstream of Protestantism, which arose on American soil — the Disciples of Christ — was to insist on a weekly observance of the Lord's Supper, but their theology of the Eucharist stressed fellowship and emphasized the memorial nature of the service. Along with the weekly Supper went a theology which insisted that man's salvation was his own very personal responsibility which he achieved by repentance and belief. The fragmentation of the religious life of the nation into many denominations was more obvious but no more harmful than the fragmentation of congregational life into a collection of individuals bent on personal salvation from hell. The two types of fragmentation go together. The insistence on individualism within the church leads to a failure of corporateness on the congregational level. Revivalism was aimed at the individual. In the revival movements that swept across the frontier periodically the individual's choices were central. He was exhorted to take his stand with Christ and place himself over against the evils of the life around him. His attitude toward the sins of the frontier — drinking, gambling, cursing, dancing — was what stamped him as a Christian, not his incorporation into the worshiping community. The Christian was a righteous man.

"The whole thrust of revivals," says Jerald C. Brauer, "was to get results in the moral life. This could be done only by converting individual souls. Thus revivalism was not concerned so much with theology or with the structure of society; it was concerned with personal morality and personal conversion." [11] Nor, it may be added, was it concerned much with the church as the body of Christ. The church was a collection of called-out individuals banded together in part at least around their moral standards, having shared in an emotional experience. The church was a prop for the individual. It helped sustain him in his quest for personal salvation. He did not hesitate to leave it when or if he no longer felt it a sustaining power. He might join with other individuals to form a new community if he found the one of which he was already a part lax in doctrinal expression or moral teaching. He continually stood in judgment on the church, read his Bible and decided whether or not the church of which he was a part measured up to his understanding of what it should be. Revivalism itself proved a divisive issue among the Presbyterians and the Congregationalists particularly. It was not an unmixed good.

It must be stressed again, however, that in its cultural framework it functioned as a vital influence in a unique way. As Professor Brauer admits:

Revivalism came to the church's rescue. It became one of the distinctive features of American Protestantism. It defeated deism and indifference, it overcame the problem of space and won thousands of members for the voluntary churches. In revivals the churches found an answer to the question of how to present the judgment and redemption of God, yet in so doing they also limited their message and bound it to emotionalism.[12]

In the influence of revivals on worship the restricted message of the revivalists carried little hint of the majesty of the church as the body of Christ into which men are privileged to enter, forming a part of a new community, marked by God's redemptive act, which is brought home to believers through the repeated process of the Word and Sacrament.

CHAPTER 11

The Beginnings of Liturgical Renewal

The religious expressions of the American frontier were to set the patterns for the worship life of the American church until well into the twentieth century. They still are the dominant influence in many segments of Protestantism. Ilion T. Jones, who is sympathetic toward what happened in the nineteenth century and who looks askance at the " liturgical revival," generalizes on the situation:

With the exception of two or three groups . . . worship may accurately be called non-liturgical or Puritan or, better still, evangelical. . . . The liturgy of the Lord's Supper has been simple but orderly with little attention to the structure of the Eucharistic prayer, with no semblance of 'sacerdotalism, and with the major emphasis on it as fellowship. Until almost the end of the nineteenth century the prevailing sentiment in most denominations was against the use of art and symbols, candles, and the like except the symbol of the cross; and even the use of the cross was violently opposed in many sections of the country; and against ceremonial and dramatic action. . . . The orders of service were simple, often informal, without the use of versicles and responses except the " Doxology " and the Gloria, with little use of prayers other than the invocation, the Lord's Prayer, the long pastoral prayer, and the benediction, and usually with a responsive reading and one scripture lection. The central act of worship was the sermon. The worship service was distinctly a preaching service with emphasis upon evangelism. Most American denominations made little or no use of the Christian year. . . . They had no books of common worship to guide their ministers and to be used as prayer books by the worshippers, and no fixed or standardized orders of service. In short, the worship of the overwhelming majority of Christian churches in the United States was of the Puritan, informal, spontaneous, spirit-filled, evangelistic type of worship of the New Testament. In short, it was evangelical worship.[1]

Dr. Jones's description may be accepted even if his conclusion is looked upon with less enthusiasm than he displays and even if the identification of the American " preaching service " with the worship of the New Testament be questioned. Actually, the Puritan, spontaneous worship of the evangelistic type had become highly liturgical. Its very informality embraced a ritual of its own, as J. Edgar Park has written:

Some kind of ritual seems necessary in all services of worship, whether it be of the " I'm a regular guy " type, " well, fellow! Here we are again! What do you say to Hymn 198? " or the solemn stereotyped Protestant form " Let us join in reading Responsive Reading number 68," or the Catholic approach to God with " Lift up your hearts," " We lift them up unto the Lord." All are equally ritual, because it is impossible to vary them every time they are used, the only difference is that the first two brothers think they are not ritualistic because what they say every Sunday is not beautiful.[2]

All worship involves liturgy, and liturgy is never an end in itself. It exists to involve the worshiper in the service and to communicate meaningfully to his needs in worship. The frontier services described in the previous chapter may well have served such a function in the environment and culture of the frontier but to transplant them to suburbia would not do. A liturgy must reflect an awareness of the environment but it must not be bound by this awareness. For part of its function is to enable man to transcend his environment, to partake of the eternal now and of the ever-present past.

When we examine the worship practices of the seventeenth and eighteenth centuries, we see the impact of the culture out of which they grew. Some of the factors in the creation of the kind of American evangelical worship Dr. Jones describes were ephemeral. They grew from political tensions. They were natural reactions against abuses found in Roman Catholic or in Anglican habits. Other factors were of deeper significance. The Reformation marked the beginning of the age of reason. Men found they could communicate truth through reasoned discourse and abstract proposition. Verbal communication gained ascendancy over more primitive means. The Protestant Church became a church wherein the sermon eclipsed all else, and the sermon was supremely a means of verbalizing truth in the seventeenth and eighteenth centuries. Theology was explained, the way of salvation was spoken that men might hear and believe. Worship was a way of speaking to and about God. There were no truths that could not be symbolized by words. This confidence in human reason made the great creeds of the Reformed churches.

Men are far less confident now of their ability to encompass by reason the realities of God and to clothe their reasoned-out comprehension in words. The Middle Ages lost the ability to communicate vital religious truth by escaping into nonverbal symbols. The post-Reformation period vigorously recaptured the importance of the verbal but by rejecting most other types of symbols tended to lose the ability to communicate other than verbally. Truth is too great to be restricted to one form, and man is too complex to be met on one level of his experience.

It was in the American church that the stripping away of so many of the traditional avenues of communication reached its height. The very vitality of American Christianity, like that of the nation itself; the scorn of things alien and aged; the evangelistic successes that gradually extended the influence of the church numerically to ever-larger segments of society, all combined to keep the denominations from examining their practices. They began to merge toward one another so that in many parts of the country only the Episcopalians stood aloof in disdainful scorn. Even the Lutherans began to abandon their tradition and become Americanized. The average main-line American church came to be rather staid, and its services were marked by a kind of solemn dignity. In lieu of vestments of the more traditional type, Protestant clergymen vested themselves in morning coats and trousers or at least in business suits of funereal black. In the latter part of the nineteenth century, architecture, unmotivated by any clearly discernible theology of worship, provided the perfect setting in a fan-shaped auditorium with a pulpit placed at the center of the platform and a background of organ pipes for bored worshipers to count. For worship in American Protestantism had come to place an intolerable load upon the preacher as a preacher.

The necessary reclamation of the sermon at the time of the Reformation infused new life into the church. But the repudiation of the worship setting for the sermon in the eighteenth and nineteenth centuries had resulted in a situation the Reformers would never have countenanced. Not only was the Eucharist disregarded, the lectionary, the church year, and the forms of prayer were lost in oblivion. Preaching was anchored in nothing deeper than the immediate interests of the preacher. Dr. Henry Sweets once satirized the practice: " I stub my toe on Tuesday, the day the bulletin goes to press, and decide to preach next Sunday on ' The Problem of Pain.' " Moreover, there was too much dependence upon the individual minister's ability as a preacher. If he failed to communicate to a particular parishioner on a given Sunday, that parishioner would probably say, " I got absolutely nothing out of church this morning."

Great preaching is the hallmark of great ages in the church. There is little excuse for the amount of poor preaching that is afforded too many congregations Sunday after Sunday. It is usually due to laziness in preparation or to sheer inability to communicate verbally. At the same time the sermon is not all there should be to a Christian service of worship and where the service as a whole is rich it lifts up the sermon to heights it may not attain when it is the central feature in a bare-bones kind of miscellany. Yet this was the kind of situation the Protestant Church backed into in the nineteenth century.

Meanwhile, a sense of what had happened in liturgy was beginning to stir the hearts and minds of many church leaders in European Protestantism. The General Assembly of the Church of Scotland as early as 1849 had appointed a committee to prepare forms of service for parishes and individuals without ministers. In 1858 the church issued a book entitled *Prayers for Social and Family Worship*. As Dr. Maxwell says: " This may seem but a slight advance, yet it denoted a remarkable change of attitude and climate; in this book the prose psalter was used, the Lord's Prayer, and Scripture lessons." [3] In 1856 the General Assembly had required the clergy henceforth to read two Scripture lessons on Sunday, one from each Testament, and had admonished its ministry to follow the Directory of Worship more closely. These were simple beginnings of movement away from the Puritan interlude, but the Church of Scotland pursued them steadily. By the first quarter of the twentieth century this church had recaptured much of its liturgical heritage. *The Book of Common Order* issued in 1940 is a splendid production, combining the Catholic tradition of Christendom with a truly Protestant and Reformed faithfulness to the essential truths of the New Testament. *The Book of Common Worship* of the Presbyterian churches in this country, published in 1946, is largely based upon it.

Scotland was not the only country in which stirring of interest in worship occurred. " The impulse toward liturgical improvement seems almost simultaneously to have taken hold of men in Reformed churches as widely scattered as those of Scotland, France, Switzerland, and the United States of America," [4] says Dr. Hageman. However, the effect of this impulse in the United States was limited and failed to touch the vast bulk of American ministers or their churches. At Mercersberg Seminary of the German Reformed Church, men of the stature of John Williamson Nevin and Philip Schaff worked out a revision of the old Palatinate liturgy which, in mangled fashion, was the liturgy of the German Reformed group. Their work was careful and deeply rooted theologically,[5] but its impact upon the other Reformed and Presbyterian churches was small.

Nevin was particularly disturbed by the lack of appreciation of the Sacraments so typical of American Protestants. Because of his teaching of a " spiritual real presence " in the Lord's Supper, he, with other members of the Mercersberg faculty, was attacked by Dr. Joseph Berg, pastor of the Race Street Reformed Church in Philadelphia. Berg, when confronted by the historical evidence, was willing to declare that both Luther and Calvin were tainted by the monstrous and prevailing dogma of transubstantiation but that fortunately their views were obsolete and those of Zwingli now prevailed throughout the Protestant world. Charles Hodge, of Princeton, entered the debate and threw the massive weight of his reputation to the side of Berg and Zwinglianism. The full effect of this controversy was not realized immediately, and the Berg-Hodge view continued to prevail generally. However, Dr. Nevin did bring to the attention of much of the scholarly world of Reformed theology the startling fact that the unsacramental character of American Protestantism was outside the mainstream of Christian tradition. He influenced individuals here and there among the leadership of other churches. Most of all, the Mercersberg group, led by Nevin and Schaff, gave the tiny German Reformed Church an Order of Worship that was theologically rooted and sacramentally oriented, and that exalted an objective, corporate service of God. Only in the past twenty-five years has the full significance of the Mercersberg movement begun to be realized and appreciated.[6]

Charles Baird, a young Presbyterian minister who preferred to remain anonymous, probably wisely, published in New York in 1855 a book entitled *Eutaxia or The Presbyterian Liturgies*. In it he reviewed the history and teachings of the Reformed churches on worship and compared them with present practices. His findings were that " the Genevan Church was early favored with a correct and well-conceived order of worship; and that order was adopted in succession by all the national Presbyterian Churches of kindred faith and discipline. . . . To this day, Great Britain and America offer the sole instances of Calvinistic churches without a Liturgy." [7] Baird pleaded for a return to the " use of those ancient, Scriptural, and Apostolic Elements of worship," for a " regular and continuous reading of Holy Scripture, at every religious service, and in sufficient portions," and for " a more strict adherence to the prescribed order of the Directory of Worship." [8] Baird had more influence in Scotland and England than he did in the United States. It was a long time before general interest in the historic liturgies of the church was to grow among Presbyterians. Tentative efforts were made here and there, but the major part of Presbyterianism in America resisted even the simplest innovations on the ground that they were Romanism in disguise.

The Roman Catholic Church meanwhile was undergoing its own liturgical renewal. The form of the Mass was set following the Council of Trent, but unrest developed here and there in the church in the nineteenth century, not as to the meaning or structure of the Mass but as to certain features within that structure. Speaking to a group of clergy and laity in a Liturgical Conference held in San Antonio, Texas, in 1959, Frank Stephen Collier stated that the " Liturgical Movement originated nowhere else than in the church of Rome. . . . It began with the rediscovery of the Gregorian chant in a reconstituted Roman abbey in France more than a century and a quarter ago." [9] A group of monks began to revive the Gregorian chants of previous centuries and in the process began to reformulate the understanding of the theology of the Mass.

The abbey was Solesmes; the leader was Dom Prosper Guéranger. The main impact of the movement was an arousal of a new sense of the primacy of worship as leaders from many parts of the Roman Church visited Solesmes and returned to their dioceses with a new sense of urgency in relation to the Eucharist. Guéranger and the monks of Solesmes were not revolutionary in any fashion. Their Mass was the orthodox formula of the Council of Trent and the Latin rite was not tampered with. It was left to a Belgian, Dom Lambert Beaudin, to advocate the translation of the Mass into the vernacular in an attempt to make participation in it, rather than in concurrent private devotions, the general practice.

In the period between the beginnings under Dom Prosper Guéranger in the middle of the nineteenth century until the recent Second Vatican Council, efforts to renew the worship life of the Roman Catholic Church recurred with regularity in various parts of Europe, particularly in France, Germany, and the Low Countries. New importance was placed upon the Word of God, read and expounded, by such men as Dom Odo Casel of the abbey of Maria Laach on the Rhineland; the importance of the Eucharist as a corporate and congregational act was stressed; and the social significance of the liturgy as hallowing all of common life was lifted up. Many Protestants reacted with surprise to recent acts of the Second Vatican Council, such as the permission given to celebrate the Mass in the vernacular at the discretion of local bishops, as though such a change was totally unrelated to the trends that had been manifest in influential Roman Catholic circles for more than a century. Behind the liturgical reforms of the council lay one hundred years of development and experimentation.

The Anglicans, always sensitive to Roman Catholic trends, were influenced in part by the experiments of their Catholic brethren, in the direction of a reevaluation of their own liturgy. They were also stirred by the decline of attendance upon the services of the Church of England. The Gothic revival in art and architecture had its influence, and the Oxford Movement made a deeper impression. Controversy ensued as the leaders of the Oxford Movement introduced into the Anglican practice ceremonies and rites directly from Roman Catholicism. The Church of England began to develop advocates of " Low " churchmanship as over against " High " churchmanship, and the point at which the conflict joined was at the point of procedure in worship.

The Oxford Movement, under the leadership of such men as E. B. Pusey, John Henry Newman, John Keble, and the other Tractarians so-called because of the series of tracts they issued endeavoring to recall the Church of England to the traditions and ceremonials of the past, had a revolutionary impact. Some of the leaders of the Oxford Movement, notably John Henry Newman, finally turned to the Roman Catholic Church, but the majority did not. Under their influence daily services were renewed in Anglican parishes, reverence and dignity were restored, and a new appreciation of the Eucharist arose in a church that had been riddled by rationalism, skepticism, and worldliness. Controversy was inevitable, and the Puseyites, as they were often called derisively, were abused in good, plain, sometimes scurrilous, nineteenth-century fashion. Horton Davies, in evaluating their influence, points to the danger inherent in their fear of liberalism, and in their dogged commitment to the inspiration of Elizabethan legislation. They also verged on " a mechanical, legalistic, and utterly impersonal idea of grace." They failed to correlate the worship life of the church with the redemptive call to the church in society. Still, when the final evaluation is made, Dr. Davies can say that " the difference in present-day attendance at the Eucharist is almost entirely due to the impact of the Oxford Movement. . . . It is hardly too much to say that the restoration of reverence to English worship is the unpayable debt that the Church of England owes to the Oxford Movement and to the Anglo-Catholics who succeeded to its mantle." [10]

The Episcopalian Church in America was drawn into the conflict and into the same kind of broad divisions of opinion and practice. The late nineteenth century saw a period of Prayer Book revision, beginning with an American revision in 1892 and spreading to England, Scotland, Canada, and South Africa by the 1920's. By that time the Americans were ready with a second revision of the Prayer Book.

On the whole the nineteenth century did not witness any great renewal in the American churches aside from the Mercersberg influence in the German Reformed Church that has already been described. The Methodists, for example, in spite of their historic tradition by way of John Wesley, were almost untouched by any movement to take that heritage seriously before well into the twentieth century. The American churches were under the influence of a revivalistic type of evangelicalism which, with its emphasis on individual salvation, fitted well the general atmosphere of the national life. There was little sense of a vital doctrine of the church anywhere in American Protestantism. The century saw the rise of great pulpit personalities – C. G. Finney, Horace Bushnell, Henry Ward Beecher, John A. Broadus, Phillips Brooks, T. de Witt Talmage, and others. These men were powerful personalities who dominated their churches and who had an immeasurable influence upon the life of the nation. It is no criticism of their contributions to the church life of the nation to say of them that they were individualists so unique that if the church were to be dependent upon their kind in her far-flung parishes, most pulpits would be empty. Furthermore, the danger inherent in the personality cult still threatens the congregational nature of the Christian church. As a writer in *The Pulpit* wrote recently: " There are still today a great number of church members who find in a Billy Graham crusade meeting all the elements of worship and nurture they have ever known: enormous choir, hearty singing, exciting preaching from a noted personality. The font and the altar are gone, but no one seems to miss them." [11]

The Eucharist almost disappeared in the nineteenth century. In a history of Alexandria, Virginia, by Mary Powell, reference is made to the Old Presbyterian Meeting House and to the Rev. Dr. Elias Harrison, who served as its pastor for forty-two years. Dr. Harrison's characteristic Sunday morning procedure is described. He "always walked slowly up the north aisle and deposited his hat and cane on the marble-topped table before mounting the pulpit steps, followed at a respectful distance by Joe Jefferson, the parish idiot, who placed his rusty hat and stick in a conspicuous place on the seat of the front pew." [12] That " marble-topped table " was the Communion table and its lost identity is symbolized by its use as a repository for the preacher's hat and cane as he passed by on his way to the pulpit. The pulpit was not just central, it was solitary. As America moved into the twentieth century, still a dominantly Protestant nation, her religious life showed flashes of genius, and her churches were vigorous. The social gospel movement was bringing a new dimension to her ethical life. Theological circles were astir, and liberalism was breaking up the unyielding, rigid patterns of the old orthodoxy. However, at the center of her life her worship was too frequently barren and narrow. The germinal seeds had been planted but had not yet borne noticeable fruit. It was left to the next generation to enter upon a " liturgical renewal."

CHAPTER 12

The Forces in Liturgical Renewal

A report of the Theological Commission of Faith and Order of the World Council of Churches issued in 1951 declared: " It is possible to discern a general trend of development which is similar in nearly all Churches — though whether this similarity is more than general and on the surface may be open to question. There is a growing sense that worship is not to be thought of as a gathering of individual pious Christians, but as a corporate act in direct relation to the Lord of the Church." [1] Individualism was the hallmark of the nineteenth century in many areas of life — in politics and social organization, in economics and in religion. The twentieth century has brought a dawning consciousness of the importance of the individual in his corporate setting. This is reflected in the welfare state, in the growth of organized labor, and in the general social atmosphere wherein the rugged individualism of the past is reflected mainly in the nostalgic slogan-mongering of conservative political movements that would repeal the twentieth century.

In religion the changed atmosphere is seen in the growing interest in a vital doctrine of the church and in the renewed appreciation on the part of Protestantism of the meaning of corporate worship. The changing social context is the basic framework within which our changing practices are to be set. Worship must unite the continuing traditions of the past with the demands of contemporary needs. As the failure to communicate to modern man in the old ways has grown more evident the church has been forced to reexamine her message and ask anew what it is she desires to communicate. This has had tremendous consequences in the field of preaching. It may be said without qualification that the methodology of preaching has changed more in the past fifty years than in the previous four hundred. Fairly clear concepts of communication through preaching have emerged, and the scope of the problem of speaking to contemporary man has been delineated by men like Fosdick, Stewart, Scherer, and Luccock. Comparable work has not emerged in the understanding of worship as the context for preaching. Much change has come about through experimentation and by intuition, but carefully developed lines of approach for those churches and churchmen whose roots go no deeper than the free-church Puritan tradition have not been available. It is true, as the Commission of the World Council asserted, that " it is possible to discern a general trend of development," but this trend has been uneven and not always informed.

The trend has been inevitable because of cultural trends, as has been indicated. It has also been inevitable because of trends within church life itself. The renewal within the Church of Rome was bound to have an effect upon Protestantism in Europe. The revival of an appreciation of the historical traditions of worship practices in Europe, particularly in England and Scotland, was bound to have an effect upon Protestantism in America. This effect began to be evident in the early decades of this century in cautious manifestations. The revival tradition was still dominant. Charles Baird's *Presbyterian Liturgies* had a limited influence in Reformed church circles. The first American Presbyterian *Book of Common Worship* was published in 1905. The Methodist Church was uneasily evaluating its frontier freedom in worship against the background of its Anglican roots. The element of Pietism continued strong enough to prevent this uneasiness from changing the general pattern of Methodism in the direction of greater formalism. However, the tentative movements toward a structured liturgy were enough to cause deep concern to the editors of *The Christian Observer*, a conservative family paper which lay next to the family Bible on the tables of many Presbyterian homes in the South. According to A. C. Piepkorn, an editorial in that journal in 1912 concluded:

The great Presbyterian churches which have so long stood as the bulwark of orthodoxy and simple worship have to all appearances abandoned the fight and are going over, piece by piece to Liberalism and ritualism." The occasion for this jeremiad was the fact that in a "conservative Presbyterian church," which the editor had attended, the first Sabbath of April had been a celebration of Easter, a cross of flowers had occupied a central place on the pulpit, and a gowned choir of twenty-four voices had entered the church in stately procession and passed out (the phrase is his) singing the recessional hymn, while in other Presbyterian churches the Apostles' Creed was being recited.[2]

What was happening to cause such consternation in the editor of *The Christian Observer*? First, there was a recognition of Easter, a tentative step toward an acceptance of the church year. In sections of this country, particularly in the South, no special observance of Easter or Christmas, as far as church services were concerned, were allowed. The Puritan Sabbath in all of its Old Testament glory and Anglo-Saxon somberness was the substitute for the Christian calendar. Secondly, the editor detected a symbol, a material symbol in the form of a cross of flowers. The plain, bare meetinghouse of the Puritan era had no room for such symbols. Further, there were symbolic actions in the processional and recessional. There were symbolic garments in the form of a vested choir. Lastly, there was the spectacle in other churches, if not in the one he attended on that first Sunday in April, 1912, of a congregation engaging in the liturgical recitation of a creedal statement. Most of the elements of the liturgical revival of the Protestant Church of the twentieth century were there in that conservative old Presbyterian church in Louisville, Kentucky.

It is not possible to cite one influence over others as being determinative of the trend. The framework was here in the new age with its decreasing *laissez-faire* philosophy which in politics and economics was to erupt into the New Deal in the 1930's. The pressures were operative already within the church, for the ecumenical movement was under way. Beginning in 1854, a series of seven interdenominational, international missionary conferences had been held, but the impact of these steps in the direction of unity had only begun to be felt in the great Edinburgh World Missionary Conference in 1910. Following this meeting, the growth of the ideal of unity was steady. The whole series of world conferences that followed and that led to the formation of the World Council of Churches had their effect in every area of church life, not least in the area of worship. The interflow of theological discussion invariably involved practices in worship. As the great communions came to know each other better their appreciation of divergent worship procedures was bound to increase. In addition, if the churches were to meet together and work together, could they not worship together? The implications of such a question created an atmosphere in which a searching reexamination of our varying worship traditions was required. This new historical consciousness led to some startling findings. The heritage of such communions as the Presbyterians and Methodists had been largely abandoned. It was revelatory to many Protestants when historical evaluation uncovered how far many of us were from the Reformers in our worship habits.

As the church moved on into the twentieth century another influence of great significance must be cited. It was the influence of those who were writing in the field of the psychology of religion. The corresponding development of a psychology of worship took place. Many Protestant ministers, vaguely aware of the inadequacy of much Protestant worship, were jolted into new insight in regard to the areas of weakness by the work of men like Willard Sperry, Von Ogden Vogt, Albert W. Palmer, Clarence Seidenspinner, and James Bissett Pratt. The basic approach of the students of the psychology of worship was not centered in history or tradition or even in Biblical teachings and practices, although the sixth chapter of Isaiah became a classic formulation of the rhythm of worship after both Sperry and Vogt, almost simultaneously but separately, discovered its pattern. The history of Christian worship was seen as " a thousand years of the process of ' trial and error.' The early church seems to have had no liturgical theory." [3] In consequence it was the responsibility of the specialist in worship to use conventional themes with " supreme skill " to create a service that would be " an artistic and literary whole, cast in a single mood and leaving at its conclusion one clear and strong impression." [4] Dr. Sperry analyzed the human needs that a service of worship should recognize and meet:

1. Praise
2. Penitence and the assurance of forgiveness
3. Thanksgiving
4. Petition
5. Intercession
6. Edification
7. Inspiration
8. Consecration
9. Benediction [5]

These concerns need to be foremost in any order of service and adjusted within the pattern of a four-part design based upon Isaiah's Temple experience — " a vision and adoration of God, a confession of creaturehood, a perception of redeeming and reconciling energy, a reaffirmation of God's glory and a rededication of the self. The first idea we may call the thesis, the second idea the antithesis, the third and fourth ideas make a final synthesis." The same pattern, said Sperry, is to be found in other Biblical passages, Ps. 42, 90, 139; John 1:1-14; I Cor., ch. 13; II Cor. 6:6-18; and Rev. 7:9-17.[6]

Von Ogden Vogt developed a seven-part pattern:

1. Vision
2. Humility
3. Vitality
4. Recollection
5. Illumination
6. Dedication
7. Peace [7]

Albert W. Palmer based his understanding upon seven great moods or life situations to which worship must minister:

1. Our need of common religious fellowship
2. Our sense of spiritual joy
3. The quest for deepening insights
4. The renewal of faith and vision
5. Our craving for comfort
6. Our need for confession and absolution
7. Our impulses toward dedication or rededication to God and to our tasks [8]

The writings of these men and of others who might be cited whose approach was much the same afforded a great contribution in the direction of a renewal of interest in a neglected field and in the direction of a framework for positive re-creation. However, their own neglect of the liturgical heritage of the church was a glaring omission, and the tendency of some writers to approach worship from a purely humanistic and psychological evaluation of man's "needs" was too great a concession to the temporary. It is true that most of these evaluations were keen and insightful, and the needs that they set forth are the perennial needs of men. Still, the somewhat cavalier fashion in which Christian tradition was overlooked left a tremendous gap in their contribution. Failure to see the place of the Eucharist as central to Christian worship was one result. Dr. Hageman summarizes it succinctly when he says that no one "in his right mind [would] want to surrender the real gains which the psychology of worship won for us. But we can lament the fact that in so many instances the first impulse to alter the traditional way of worship in the Reformed churches came from a psychology that had little or no theological orientation." [9] Nor, it may be added, did the psychology of worship reveal very much historical orientation.

The psychologist cannot be blamed for the failure of the churchman to give his valid contributions a theological and a historical framework. James B. Pratt had warned in *The Religious Consciousness* that "the attempt to produce merely subjective religious effects is always in danger of defeating itself. For religion . . . involves a belief which means to have objective validity." [10] Ten years later Dr. Pratt was to be even more emphatic as, writing on the *Eternal Values in Religion*, he says:

For the sake of clear exposition it may be well to call the psychological aspect of devotion subjective worship, and to use the phrase objective worship to indicate the act of the soul conceived of as an objective transaction between the individual and the divine Other. Using the terms in this sense we must now say that subjective worship has indeed its place: that we are justified in aiding others and aiding ourselves by all sorts of arrangements, both physical and psychical, in bringing about a state of mind in which worship shall be possible and natural. But if worship be taken as subjective only it necessarily defeats itself. Subjective worship to be successful depends upon objective worship.[11]

The clergyman was not listening to the warnings of men like Pratt, Sperry, and others. He was only lifting from the work of the expert in the field of the psychology of religion techniques and approaches that in themselves were dangerously incomplete until wedded to sound historical insights and significant theological affirmations.

The result has often been seen in efforts to seek impressive forms of worship. Aesthetic tastes led to architectural changes, music improvement, greater dignity and solemnity. Not always were worship committees and ministers informed as to what they were doing or why they were doing it. The liturgical revival has threatened at times to become an extravagant venture into the bizarre. Mood creation became the sole purpose of some worship accouterments. The dimming of overhead lights, the judicious use of spotlights, the soft playing of the organ to cover the squeak in the deacon's shoes as the offering was being received — these and manifold other features of greater or lesser importance came to reflect an appreciation of the psychology of worship. However, it was usually the *minister's* appreciation that such changes reflected, and it was *his* tastes and interests that determined the changes. There was little attempt to lead the laity into an understanding of the modifications of the order of worship. There were few efforts to instruct the laity as to the nature of Christian worship or the resources available to deepen and enhance our Protestant services, not just along aesthetic lines, but by an appropriation of a heritage that is rightfully ours. Even in those churches where liturgical procedures were introduced the service was still the minister's, with auxiliary aid from the choir. The basic need to make Christian worship a more completely congregational act was not realized very often.

Fortunately, the superficiality of the liturgical renewal of the period between World War I and World War II is not the whole story by any means. The new and broadening interchange among the denominations influenced by the ecumenical movement opened up new areas of sharing and mutual exchange. The United Church of Canada, formed in 1925 through union of the Presbyterian, Methodist, and Congregational Churches, created a Eucharistic rite that combined features of the Scottish Presbyterian, the Scottish Episcopalian, the English Anglican rites plus modifications from Congregational and Methodist uses. The result is a most effective and meaningful liturgy. The rite of the Church of South India has followed the classic structure of the liturgy in such a way that Lutherans, Presbyterians, Anglicans, and Methodists can all give wholehearted support. These successful interdenominational experiments in liturgical matters have afforded an example for the whole church and have made an impression upon American Protestantism. They have helped move us from a purely psychological approach to worship toward an examination of the traditions of the church. We discover there those practices which, combined with Biblical principles, can offer guidance in a somewhat confused area.

As we stand now it would appear that the real liturgical renewal is just beginning for most Protestant groups in America. The tentative beginnings in the nineteenth century were limited in their effects. The whole field of psychology with its implications for worship certainly jarred the church in general into an awareness of the need for reform. The studies in the history of worship that have been written in recent years have begun to reach the parish minister and he is aware, if his people are not, of the betrayal of the church's heritage that has occurred. Biblical research has had its consequences for worship. A new appreciation of the oneness of Word and Sacrament has come about. Protestantism's separation of the two and its exaltation of the Word spoken apart from the Word acted in the Sacrament is unbiblical.

The question now is, Where do we go? What do we accept from the past and what do we reject? What principles can guide us into the renewal of the church's worship? How can the tension be maintained between objectivity and subjectivity in worship in such a way that the extremes of medieval spectator worship can be avoided without lapsing into the kind of interior sponge bath evoked by " I Come to the Garden Alone "? Are we forced to choose between what J. S. Whale has called the "Protestant Word-Service" on the one hand, and the "Roman Catholic Mystery-Service " on the other? Our historical survey should have thrown some light by indirection at least on some answers to these questions. The essential feature of the answer begins to emerge if we see worship as the combining of the enduring with the temporal, the merging of the traditional into contemporary forms of expression in such a way that the Christian message in its unchanging validity is communicated, so that modern man in his ephemeral setting is reached and involved.

CHAPTER 13

Present Emphases in Liturgical Renewal

The study of the history of worship for the sake of the study itself can be fruitless. John H. S. Kent has written:

Antiquarianism in worship has been handicapping Christianity throughout the past hundred and fifty years. The very name of the Liturgical revival implies the assumption, rarely questioned, that if only we could decide how people worshipped in such and such a past century we should have discovered the kind of worship which we ought to imitate today. As a result, liturgical experiment is too often dominated by liturgical scholarship and there is produced, not a twentieth-century liturgy expressing what twentieth-century worshippers have to say, but a twentieth-century academic impression of what the Early Church may be supposed to have done. The results are more satisfying to ministers than people.[1]

Aside from wishing that the last sentence of the above quotation had read " to ministers than *other* people," there is nothing with which one can disagree in Dr. Kent's statement. However, the situation he describes is more true of England and Scotland than it is of the United States. Antiquarianism has not handicapped the churches of America as much as a lack of a sense of the past. Now that the books on the history of worship have multiplied and some familiarity with the traditions of the past may be assumed, the problem of the proper balance of past and present confronts us. It is important to remember that the church has again and again adapted her practices to the age in which she found herself. The world of the first-century church was a world in which the practices of synagogue and temple as a vehicle for the faith were largely effective. As it moved into a larger world of varied cultures more variety of procedure was inevitable. The major break in worship patterns came, according to Dom Gregory Dix, when the private community worship of the fellowship of believers became the public worship of the Roman state after Constantine. Ceremonial increased as the Middle Ages arrived, the ceremonial of the church only reflecting the elaborateness of the culture. As the Renaissance made its impact and as the Reformation came the church reflected the new society with worship practices that were increasingly intellectualized and dependent upon verbal forms of communication. This process reached its apex in the modified Puritanism of the free churches of the American continent. There is no single liturgical norm in terms of structure and order. However there are norms around which any Christian service of worship should evolve if it is to maintain its meaning as Christian.

The Christian worships God through Jesus Christ our Lord, and theologically his worship depends upon the doctrine of incarnation. The worship of the church celebrates the incarnation, affirms it and rejoices in it. Through the centuries the Christian calendar grew up as a pattern within which the worship of the church was drawn back again and again to celebrate the central events of the incarnation theology — Advent, Epiphany, Lent, Pentecost. In the cycle of the Christian year worshipers were reminded of the coming of God in Christ and of the death of Christ for man's sake. Central to Christian worship for most of the centuries of the church's life was the Eucharist. Here the worshiper is reminded of the central meaning of the incarnation. It is impossible to discern the full significance of all the theological vagaries of the meaning of the Lord's Supper. What did it mean exactly to the early church? For Oscar Cullmann, the primitive Lord's Supper gravitates

around "two poles; the presence of Christ and the fellowship of those who experience that presence . . . the joy
manifested by the early Christians during the ' breaking of
bread ' has its source, not in the fact that the assembled disciples eat the body and drink the blood of their Crucified
Master, but in the consciousness they have of eating *with*
the Risen Christ, really present in their midst, as He was on
Easter Day." [2] By the Middle Ages the idea of eating the
body and drinking the blood of the crucified Master was so
elaborated and embroidered as to give substance to a doctrine of transubstantiation. The reaction of the Reformers
ranged from Zwingli's stress on the memorial aspects of the
Supper to Luther's doctrine of consubstantiation. The point
to note is that from the very early days of the church until
the eighteenth century the celebration of the Lord's Supper
was the focus of Christian worship. Any liturgical renewal
which ignores this focal point is breaking ties with the past
to a dangerous degree.

Does the Lord's Supper communicate reality in the twentieth century? It does not if it is made to bear the burden
of past theological dogmas which do not speak to the twentieth century. We cannot revive the pristine eschatological
faith of the early Christians who celebrated the past, present, and future coming of their Lord in simple, realistic
manner. Certainly the Protestant cannot accept any doctrine of Real Presence that involves transubstantiation. He
can, however, see in this impregnation of bread and wine by
the Spirit of God a Real Presence as a symbol of the incarnation. Remembering the sacrifice of our Lord, he can see
more than the memorial of his death at the Table of Communion. He can see the whole significance of his coming,
then in Galilee and now in a confused, broken world. He
can see the symbol of wholeness amid brokenness, of recon-
ciliation in fraction. The Communion is not a static but an
active symbol. It is a dramatized presentation of Christian
faith.

Dom Gregory Dix makes much of the difference between the conception of the Eucharist today as something *said* and the conception of the Eucharist before the fourth century as something *done*.[3] The distinction is not unimportant, for when the Eucharist is conceived to be something said, the congregation comes to hear. When it is something done, the congregation comes to share in the doing. As a truly corporate act of a worshiping group of Christians the Lord's Supper becomes more meaningful. The Presence becomes a Real Presence, not in the old simplistic sense, but in a vivid sense; not in a spatial, temporal sense but in an actual sense as, through handling the material elements of bread and wine, the Divine Reality becomes real through faith. The dualism between " spirit " and " body " is destroyed, and some sense of a sacramental universe is restored. For, as Donald Baillie says:

We must believe that when Christianity took the common elements of water and bread and wine and made sacraments of them, it was because this universe is the sacramental kind of place in which that can fitly happen; because these elements, these creatures of God, do lend themselves to such a use; and because we men and women, who are another sort of God's creatures, do require in our religion such a use of material things and symbolic actions.[4]

We bring bread to be shared in the name of Christ, bread which is the stuff of ordinary life, the staff of daily existence. Because we meet Christ and commune with one another in the sharing of the bread at the Table of the Lord's Supper, we symbolize the fact that we can meet him wherever bread is shared. Communion among men can take place around any table because we remind ourselves again and again of the fact of Communion around the table at which a worshiping congregation gathers. We bring wine to be shared in the name of Christ (though most Protestants in this country use grape juice, a custom that grew out of the temperance movements of the last century). Here is the fruit of the vine, given of God, often used by man to degrade and destroy himself, the very stuff of ecstasy and symbol of the extraordinary. In the sharing of wine we represent the coming of God into all human experience, the joyful and the ecstatic as well as the commonplace and plain. Bread and wine are hallowed, and in the light of their hallowing we see that all of life is touched by the goodness of God. There is a Real Presence in the Eucharist and therefore there is a Real Presence everywhere. Thus the sacrament remains, even in the twentieth century, a sign and seal.

Surely here is a theological approach that speaks to the mind of our scientific, materialistic age while retaining the ageless dramatic action of the church in its celebration of the coming of God in the very material flesh and blood of a man. This dramatic action is apt to be meaningless if it is allowed to continue out on the fringes of Protestant practice. Dr. Gossip paraphrases some words of Thomas à Kempis in regard to Communion, " If this were only to be had in one place, once a year, how folk would stream to it! But because any one can have it anywhere, we turn in to it as to a commonplace affair of no particular account." [5] Perhaps! But the experience of the bulk of American Protestants has not been in support of Thomas à Kempis' cry. He lived in an age when the celebration of the Mass occurred at every turn. We live at the end of an age when for most of Protestantism the Communion of the Lord's Supper has been infrequent. Many of our parishioners stay away on Communion Sunday, slightly bored if they come and vaguely uneasy in a service they do not understand. The Presbyterians, the Methodists, and the Baptists have been most guilty at the point of the displacement of the Eucharist.

Any endeavor to return to weekly observances in the churches of these denominations would meet widespread resistance. The claim would be made that weekly Communion is impractical and unnecessary. There is the fear that too frequent celebration would cause the Supper to slip to the level of a gesture. That it has retained its significance not only for Episcopalians and Roman Catholics but for the extremely free-church Disciples of Christ should give pause to those who advance this argument. Nonetheless, the possibility of weekly celebration for most American Protestant groups would appear unlikely at present. The recent *Service for the Lord's Day and Lectionary for the Christian Year*, published under the sponsorship of The Joint Committee on Worship of The United Presbyterian Church in the United States of America and the Presbyterian Church in the United States, makes provision for the probability that the service of Communion will not be held each week but it does so with an admonition to "frequent observance" and so structures the service that it is plain that the Eucharist is not an addition to the public worship of the congregation but a normal culmination of that worship.[6] Certainly we need to consider a more frequent celebration than the quarterly observance that is common practice. At least the celebration of the Sacrament of the Lord's Supper may fittingly take place on days of special significance such as Maundy Thursday, the beginning of Advent, and Ash Wednesday.

The report of the World Council Commission of Faith and Order distinguished three views regarding the relative priority of Word and Sacrament:

(*a*) The substance of the worship is to be found in the sermon to which the Sacrament is an addition, a confirmation of the promise given in the proclamation of the Word; indeed there are many for whom a Eucharist without a sermon is a torso, an illegitimate divorcing of the ministry of the Sacrament from the ministry of the Word;

(*b*) the Sacrament is the substantial act of worship: the reading and preaching of the Gospel as part of the whole liturgy heralds the coming presence of the Lord, and brings the challenge of that presence to the world;

(*c*) sermon and Sacrament are complementary. The Sacrament is upheld by, and is the bringing to life of, our Lord's words of institution; the sermon, in which God Himself addresses the congregation, though through frail human channels, is an action by means of which God's grace reaches man.[7]

The weight of Christian tradition would seem to support the third position: " sermon and Sacrament are complementary." Because the Sacrament had been separated from the Word in the medieval church and because it was celebrated in a way that excluded the congregation except as spectators, the Reformers were prone to insist that the complementary nature of sermon and Sacrament required that neither was to be celebrated without the other. In our age when Communion in Protestant churches is celebrated in the vernacular and when the Words of Institution always accompany it, it may well be that the time has come to re-examine this phase of Protestant tradition. There are dangers in its abandonment, to be sure, but the danger on the other side of the practical elimination of the Eucharist from our preaching services has proved to be greater.

When worship is something *said*, the congregation comes to *hear*. Whether it be a said Mass or a sermon with prayers said by the minister and responses sung by the choir, the congregation comes to hear. When worship is something *done*, the congregation comes to *take part*. This principle applies not only to the Eucharist, but to the service of the spoken Word. In the Eucharist greater congregational participation may be symbolized if the elements are brought forward by the officers, if the congregation comes forward to receive them rather than to be served seated in their pews. In the service of the spoken Word greater congregational participation can be afforded through the use of collects and litanies, through the symbol of kneeling for prayer, and through the restoration to the people of the " Amen " as a response. It is striking that the result of the radical worship reform of the post-Reformation period was to deprive the worshipers of the participation that the Reformation itself had restored to them.

One of the basic objections of the Reformers to the worship of the Middle Ages came at the point of the exclusion of the congregation from the acts of worship. The prayers were offered by the priests at the altar, the responses were given by his helpers and by the choir, the elements were offered to the congregation in only one form. Luther took the worship in song away from the great choirs of medieval times and restored it to the congregation. Both he and Calvin encouraged congregational responses and the use of unison prayers. Thus the movement toward fragmentation of the congregation into a group of individuals at their private devotions while the Mass was being celebrated by the priests at the altar was counteracted. As the Protestant groups moved into the seventeenth century they began to become preacher-centered in the same way the Roman Catholic Church had been priest-centered. Although congregational singing continued to be one of the strong features of Protestant church life, other acts of congregational involvement dropped away. The Doxology was omitted, the Apostles' Creed and the Lord's Prayer fell into disuse. The prayers of the minister grew longer and longer. It is said that Samuel Whiting, of Lynn, Massachusetts, one of New England's early divines, used to preach for an hour and a half, followed immediately by a prayer at least thirty minutes in length. We cannot say that the congregations did not participate vicariously in such prayers and sermons. So involved were these people in their faith that the worship practices they shared may well have caught them up into corporate oneness.

The features were there, nevertheless, that were to dissolve that oneness. Increasingly, Protestant worship came to depend upon the personality of the minister and his effectiveness or ineffectiveness in verbally lassoing his congregation into worship. In more recent times the choir has become a feature of worship to be enjoyed when their musical offering to God or to the congregation was impressive, and to be criticized when it was not impressive. No longer is it a support and guide to the congregation of which it is a part but, in many churches, an act or an entertainment bill on which the minister is given top billing. Some churches carry an announcement " Special Music " somewhere in the order of service. This means that the choir does not know what it will sing but it will decide at the last-minute rehearsal just before church after the director sees who is present. Something must be sung or the congregation will be disappointed! This is not intended as sarcasm but as a simple description of factual events that most of us will recognize. Surely the devotion and invaluable service of multitudes of choir members can be acknowledged while at the same time a word of rebuke is given to the manner in which we have allowed that devotion and service to be distorted. The choir is intended to be a part of the congregation, assuming the very vital function of supporting and leading the congregation in singing, and in offering unto God on behalf of the congregation appropriate praise in music not fitted for group participation by the congregation as a whole. It is not intended to act instead of the congregation in responding to the minister's prayers on behalf of all with "Amen." Congregational responses should be reintroduced into our services of worship.

Some churches are providing the worshipers with the books of worship of their respective traditions for pew use. This is a helpful step in the direction of creating anew the sense of corporate worship as a congregational act. This means that the prayers that are suited for unison usage may be cited in the church bulletin and prayed by the entire gathering. It means that the liturgy of the church can be made familiar to the laity through use. Dr. Hageman finds it a "healthy sign" that this kind of procedure is being encouraged by all of the newer liturgies, especially in Europe.

Both the French and the Dutch liturgies, for example, contain congregational responses to almost every part of the service. In fact, the Dutch Dienstboek even prints the musical settings for the responses with the liturgical texts. Such service books are really *liturgies*, providing for the work of the people. We need to think of our service books in this way and not as manuals and guidebooks for the minister only.[8]

We have long accepted the congregation's active participation in the hymns but for most congregations, participation has ended there. Yet the weight of tradition and the implications of our understanding of the nature of the church would lead us to see that the congregation's participation in worship must extend to an identification of the group in prayer, in the Eucharist, in the Scripture, and even in the sermon. The worship experience is the highest expression of the total corporate life of the church. When worship becomes the province of the minister exclusively, the corporate life is bereft of its highest meaning. Our worship must express what the twentieth century has to say in terms that carry the insights of the ancient gospel. Our worship is our greatest witness. It is a corporate witness, and we need to restore a sense of corporateness in the witness of worship to our highly individualized collections of people.

The Eucharist and the people — here are two needed emphases in Christian worship: the Eucharist at the heart of the church's life and the people at the place where the Eucharist is celebrated as involved partakers in the act of Communion. The Liturgy of the Word interpreted through the reading of the Scripture, the prayers, and the sermon, remains distinctively Protestant as an emphasis. No careful student of the history of the church would denigrate it. However, when it stands alone, as it so often does, overshadowing the Liturgy of the Lord's Supper to the point of extinction and violating the doctrine of the priesthood of believers by depreciating the participation of the congregation, reform is imperative.

CHAPTER 14

The Word in Tradition and in Symbols

One clear mark of the liturgical renewal of the twentieth century has been the move to place greater stress upon the celebration of the Communion of the Lord's Supper with greater regularity than was customary in most Protestant denominations in this country a century ago. The process of congregational participation in the acts of worship through a more widespread use of litanies and collects, through unison prayers of confession and affirmations of faith, has grown apace. Few Protestants find objections to either of these two trends, although the stubbornly free-church adherent would protest any use of set forms of prayer. With other developments in public worship in many churches in recent decades, there is less readiness of acceptance. Many people look upon the multiplication of symbolism with suspicion and uncertainty. Our heritage is one that has repudiated the use of material symbols as popish. The abuses against which the Puritans protested were real, and the violence of their reactions understandable.

A continuing violent rejection of useful and traditional symbols is less understandable. We know more now about the way in which people learn than our forefathers did. We do not rely as completely upon the spoken word as the sole instrument for the conveyance of knowledge as did former generations. There are certain symbols that speak a universal tongue. Color is one. Psychologists have taught us what color can do. Some colors lift the heart. Other colors have a somber effect upon human feelings. Some colors are stimulating. Other colors act as sedatives to the spirit. Children go to school in rooms painted in yellow, green, and similar colors that give a lilt to the heart, an unconscious lilt but no less important because the attitude is not verbalized. Color is an elemental mode of communication. For centuries the church has used color symbolism. White is a joyous color and appropriately enough was used for weddings, baptisms, Christmas, and Easter. Green is an expansive color and was used for the period of Epiphany, expressive of the universal meaning of our Lord. Purple and violet are somber hues and have been used for the seasons of Advent and Lent, periods of penitence and preparation. Red is a color evoking violence and passion. It has been associated with Pentecost and the strong manifestations of the Holy Spirit. Black is the obvious sign of mourning. On only one day of the Christian year was it used in the church's worship, and that was Good Friday in memorial of the black despair of the crucifixion.

There is an appropriateness in communicating the moods of the church by means of color. The use of a fittingly colored parament, or pulpit scarf, and Bible marker, the donning of the proper stole or vestment — these symbols can say something without words, using one of the most primitive modes of expression. Although primitive, the use of color is also highly refined. The artist makes it his instrument; the psychologist interprets its importance. Man needs to worship with his whole being. He responds to life with taste, feeling, touch, seeing, with his instincts as well as with his hearing. He responds to life unconsciously and absorbs understanding from his surroundings. Color symbols may need to be explained to the average congregation but once they have become a part of the general atmosphere of worship they communicate their own message and help create their own effect.

Another symbol that can enrich Protestant worship is

the use of the church year. Again, in fairness to the Puritans, it must be said that their rejection of the elaborate calendar of the medieval church was a creative and necessary step. The year was filled with feast days, dedicated to martyrs and saints without number. On the high festival days, such as Christmas, ribaldry and revelry abounded. Such celebrations were stretched out to last as long as possible. Merry England was given over to drunkenness, gluttony, and dissipation during the "twelve days of Christmas." The social conditions of the times were responsible for the feeling of the need for such bacchanalian revels. The revels existed nonetheless. The Puritans recoiled in justifiable scorn from such distortions of the real good news of God's redemptive act in Jesus Christ. Unwisely, they abolished any recognition of the Christian calendar. Where they were in power, they attached penalties to such recognition. The General Court of Massachusetts in 1659 passed a law forbidding anyone to "keep Christmas." The law declared that "anybody who is found observing by abstinence from labor, feasting or in any other way any such days as Christmas day, shall pay for every such offence, five shillings."

The early Reformers had not gone so far. Luther had retained the major festivals of the Christian year, and Calvin had called for the observance of Christmas, Good Friday, Easter, Ascension Day, and Whitsunday or Pentecost. At a later time, when Methodism was founded, Wesley, in accord with Anglican tradition, had adhered to the Christian year. Yet it was not the Reformation or Wesleyan practice that obtained in the American churches with the exception of the liturgical groups such as the Lutherans and the Episcopalians. As was true in other areas, it was the Puritan tradition that triumphed and came to be identified with the beliefs and practices of the Reformers. Europe for centuries was rooted in the Christian year. Her culture reflected its existence and her social life was organized around its framework. In our increasingly secular-oriented society the church would do well to lift up before her people with renewed emphasis the great pivotal days of the Christian calendar. They serve as recurring reminders of the mighty acts of God in history — Advent, the passion and resurrection of our Lord, the coming of the Holy Spirit at Pentecost.

Strangely enough, churches that recognize secular holidays such as Mother's Day, Independence Day, Memorial Day, and Labor Day find the days of ecclesiastical emphasis out of place. William M. Ramsey, writing in the *Presbyterian Outlook*, recalls a professor who related a story of the furor raised in his childhood in a certain Southern Presbyterian church by someone's putting a bowl of flowers in the church on Easter. The basis for the objection was the fear that the recognition of Easter was a first step toward popery. Dr. Ramsey also remembers how in his own experience of but a few years ago in southwestern Kentucky, Southern Baptist ministers were willing to join in " pre-Easter revivals " but were hesitant to cooperate in " Holy Week Services." [1] Although the Southern Presbyterian Church added " Easter " to its official calendar in 1951, a motion before the General Assembly to include Advent, Epiphany, and Lent in the denominational calendar was defeated a few years later. The argument from the floor centered on the fear that such a move was dangerously liturgical and that a recognition of the church calendar would smother the spontaneity of preaching and the freedom of worship.

One may counter that disciplined appropriation of the main events of the Christian story and a confrontation of the church with the ever-renewed significance of these events may be one way whereby we keep returning to the essential gospel. In the church calendar is a splendid symbol of God's claim upon time and eternity. Advent affords solemn preparation for the coming of our Lord at Christmas. It reminds us of God's relation to history. Christmas is the affirmation of the incarnation. Epiphany, with its remembrance of the myth of the Magi, represents the beginning of the season of Christ's universal unveiling to all mankind. Lent, like Advent, is a time of solemn preparation for the depths of the passion and the heights of Easter Day. The forty days after Easter until Ascension Sunday offer the opportunity for stress upon the living and ever-present Christ. Pentecost symbolizes the coming of the Holy Spirit and the beginning of Trinitytide season, which was " open " to those emphases necessary to round out the life of the church. From the standpoint of worship, the Christian calendar offers a framework within which the total story of God's self-revelation can be encompassed. For the preacher, it offers a pull back again and again to the major proclamations of the gospel. To the world it affords a witness, reminding all men over and over of an Advent, a passion, and a resurrection. There need be no lack of freedom within this framework, no smothering of initiative within this structure. As Charles W. F. Smith has said:

The men and women in the congregation can be protected from the limitations and idiosyncrasies of the preacher by an orderly and cyclical plan that imposes upon the preacher some element of authority, control, or guidance, but is not in itself a strait jacket. The fear of killing the preacher's freedom and spontaneity has been greatly exaggerated. Where spontaneity exists (as a welcome discovery in place of the use of canned material), it is too hardy and vigorous to be thus easily destroyed.[2]

In addition to the rediscovery of the centrality of the Eucharist and the reinvolvement of the congregation in the acts of worship, the use of color symbolism and the reestablishment of the ecclesiastical calendar are aspects of the liturgical renewal to which Protestant churches may well give attention. What of other ancient symbols of the church? There is no use in reintroducing symbols simply because they are ancient. The Eucharist can stand the acid tests of modernity. So can the Christian calendar. Some symbols from the past cannot. An indiscriminate use of the ancient lectionary may obscure the Christian message. Some psalms in the lectionary carry sub-Christian themes that the alert Christian today would find difficult to accept as Scripture. Many of the Old Testament passages and some of the New Testament selections can baffle and dismay when read without comment as the " Lesson " for the day. Our view of prophecy has changed so that we no longer see the predictive passages of the Old Testament writers in the same infallible light. Psalm 2, for example, is part of the evening lectionary for the first Sunday after Christmas in the Presbyterian *Book of Common Worship*. The Old Testament lesson for the same date is from the majestic fortieth chapter of Isaiah and the New Testament lesson is the incomparably beautiful and tender second chapter of Luke. Psalm 2 was once believed to be predictive of the coming of Christ, and the somewhat ominous twelfth verse, " Kiss the Son, lest he be angry, and ye perish from the way, when his wrath is kindled but a little," was conceived as an expression of Christ's function as judge. What Biblical scholar would hold this interpretation today? The psalm celebrates the enthronement of an Israelitish king who is spoken of as a son of the Lord and to whom obeisance must be given. The psalm no longer has the meaning for the church that it once had and to use it as a lesson for Christmastide is legalistic obscurantism.

The Bible may well be read more than it has been in the average Protestant church. The practice of selecting a brief passage from which the sermon will be launched has been too common. The renewed practice of reading more than one lesson is to be commended. The reverent attention given to the Bible and its place of prominence in worship are symbols of its importance to the Protestant faith. The reading of both Old and New Testament lessons highlights this importance. Interestingly enough, it has been in recent years that the custom of more than one Scripture lesson has renewed itself. The stanchly conservative men of the eighteenth century with their sturdy belief in a verbally inspired Bible looked askance upon the reading of Scripture in public. Maxwell says of the Scottish church in this period, " The statements that Holy Scripture was not read at all in the services are often, but certainly not always, exaggerated — one group read them *simpliciter,* and the other group interspersed an exposition. There were many, however, who read very little indeed — a few verses — and probably none read the chapter from each Testament recommended by the Directory." [3] The Bible was thought to be the center of worship at home. To read it in public took time from prayers and from preaching. " As late as 1857 such expressions as this were commonly heard: ' The reading of the Bible in church is a mere waste of time — we can read our Bibles at home.' " [4]

There are many ancient practices of the church that should be carefully considered in the light of the twofold principle of authentic tradition and contemporary meaning. Such minor usages as the placing of candles in the sanctuary area can cause controversy. There is certainly no point in placing candles in the church because they are pretty and have romantic associations. There is even less point in placing them in the chancel and leaving them unlighted Sunday after Sunday. Unlighted candles are a negative symbol. Yet they adorn Communion tables in many Protestant churches I have been in.

The use of vestments is another minor symbol that can arouse debate.

A vested clergy came about by accident. There was no special clerical garb for the first four centuries of church history. As the daily garments of the citizens of the Roman Empire underwent great style changes the clergy continued to wear the clothing of the conservative Roman gentlemen. When even the conservative gentlemen changed, it was characteristic of the clergy that they resisted. Gradually the long cassock became a distinguishing mark of the priest. For various reasons additions were made to clerical garb until it became distinctive and unique. There is nothing holy about the special clothing of the priest or minister. Neither is there anything unholy and subversive in distinctive garb. *The Christian Century*'s " Quintus Quiz " of some years ago once quoted a wise old teacher as saying of preachers that there were two kinds with which he had no patience: those who thought it a matter of first principle to wear clerical dress and those who thought it a matter of first principle not to wear clerical dress. Vestments or no vestments is an issue that should be decided on a functional basis. By and large, even the most conservative Protestant churches have accepted vestments for their choirs. Actually, they have long lived with vested clergymen. Sometimes the vestment was a funereal black suit with matching tie. For many in the last generation it was a morning coat with striped trousers. Increasingly, it has been a Genevan scholar's gown. A growing practice among Methodists and Presbyterians has been the use of the clerical collar and vest, not only for pulpit wear but in the pursuit of pastoral responsibilities. There is much to be said for this practice in our increasingly impersonal, highly urbanized society. It affords immediate identification and is a symbol of function. There is a subtle psychological difference in the hospital call made by a minister upon a parishioner when the minister is dressed in a business suit or tweeds and when he is dressed in clerical garb. This is especially true where the relationship is tenuous between the minister and his parishioner. Clerical clothing helps to give an immediate framework to the relationship. The effect may be subtle but it is real, and the writer has experienced it on numerous occasions.

The argument is often advanced that special garb sets the minister off from his people and helps to create the idea of a special priestly caste. A collar never sets a man off from other people. It is the man within the collar who creates the gulf if there is one. The collar may be round or button-down Ivy League. If by voice and demeanor the minister within the collar proclaims his apartness, people hear the proclamation. How many of us know fiercely free-church ministers in sack suits and bright neckties who announce with their opening words that they are " preachers," not by direct statements but by tone of voice and inflection, even by bearing. On the other hand, how many of us know men in clerical vest who could fit graciously into any company and allow people to remain at ease because of a feeling that this man of God was a person who respected them as persons.

The reasons for dealing with such secondary symbols as candles and vestments is to illustrate the point that the liturgical renewal of our age requires an appreciation of the ancient customs of the church and an examination of their possible meaning for us. There is always a danger of becoming lost in the secondary. The Anglican Church, after the vigor infused into it by the Oxford Movement of the early nineteenth century, then became lost in the elaborate details of ceremonial in the late nineteenth century. There was violent controversy over bowing to the crucifix, the burning of incense, the use of holy water and numerous other garnishments. It is to be hoped that the present interest of Protestants in their procedures in worship will not lose sight of the very meaning of Christian worship, which is the celebration of our relationship to God in Christ and a renewal of its meaning for all of life. Ancient customs may continue to be helpful. Certainly they maintain a sense of the continuity of the faith but they must be continually examined lest they become fetishes. New customs must be introduced when and where they express authentic apprehension of the meaning of God for life today. It is important neither to be bound nor to be so completely free as to worship in a vacuum void of the traditional.

Worship is a total affair. Surroundings contribute to its meaning. The minor aspects of the setting in which worship occurs are important. Week after week they contribute to the impact that is made. A Christian congregation can worship in a field or a theater or a barn, but that is because of prior associations. Should three or even two generations of Christians worship in a field or a theater or a barn completely separated from other settings, the result would be a complete revolution in the psychology of worship. Through the years, impact is made upon the conscious and the unconscious mind by a complex variety of associations. The effect is cumulative. The associations become interwoven with the emotional texture of life. As important as direct instruction in religious values is, direct instruction cannot stand alone. It becomes meaningful as it is interpretative of experiences, emotional and volitional experiences. "We love, because he first loved us." (I John 4:19.) So we understand because we have first felt. We experience God in worship, and we see reality in symbolic form. Word symbols are the most sophisticated form by which reality is conveyed, but they are not the only form. Usually they build upon fundamental relationships and associations already created. If worship makes use of appropriate symbols to create warmth, beauty, acceptance, and concern, the words of Bible and sermon interpreting God in these terms go home to the heart more readily. If worship is barren, abstract, ungainly, it is difficult to offset these associations by words. Light, color, the many colors in stained-glass windows, the cross — these are representative symbols the church has found effective in establishing the fundamental relationships and the basic associations by which meaning is conveyed. "Society lives by its symbols," says Amos N. Wilder.

The cross is one thing, and the Swastika is another. The Sheaf of Wheat is one thing, and the Fasces is another. The "Battle Hymn of the Republic" speaks one faith and the "Internationale" another. The Lincoln Memorial and tomb of Lenin evoke and nourish mutually exclusive images of mankind.[5]

The church, too, lives by her symbols. She cannot live without them. If she attempts to confine them to verbal symbols and to rational creedal statements or to represent her faith in terms of moral laws and to depend upon the arousing of subjective emotions as a substitute for total personal response and involvement, she will not live as a vital part of twentieth-century man's culture very long.

CHAPTER 15

Renewal Through Worship

Man must use symbols in his worship. After Puritanism had reduced the symbols of the church almost exclusively to verbal symbols and to an architecture that symbolized a rejection of ritual and the arts, the renewal of an interest in other forms of symbolism was inevitable as a reaction. It was slow in coming in the American church because of the efficacy of Puritanism in large segments of our population. There was a sense in which Puritan forms met the needs of our rapidly expanding, activistic, moralistic community life in which little attention was given to most of the arts. When other forms of symbolism began to enter our church life, they were sometimes far worse than the simple Puritan forms. The graceful, plain meetinghouse, for example, had been an authentic architectural expression of a simple, rational faith. The church architecture of the late nineteenth century was for the most part grotesque, culminating in the fantastic Akron plan, born in 1867 and until well into the twentieth century destined to clutter the landscape with church buildings that expressed nothing very clearly. When art came back to the Protestant churches, it came in the form of grossly sentimental paintings of a feminine Jesus cuddling lambs, culminating in the folk-hero Jesus of Sallman's *Head of Christ*. It was bad art and superficial religion.

Too deep an engrossment in the contemporary may lead

to shallow expressions in both liturgy and symbolism. Many churches discard the Apostles' Creed, for example, and use some modern expression of belief. Many of these modern creeds are good statements and should be used upon occasion. Still, ours is not a creed-making age. Most of our attempts at creedal statement reflect their very temporary nature. Few of them convey the thrill of authentic Christian conviction to a congregation. There are problems with the Apostles' Creed. Many people cannot take some of its statements literally. Yet if it is seen for what it is — a tie with more than a millennium of Christian affirmation and a symbol of the communion of the saints — it comes alive and one feels with Studdert-Kennedy that it ought to be said "standing at spiritual attention with the roll of drums in your ears, the light of love dazzling your eyes, and all the music of a splendid world crashing out a prelude to its truth." [1]

That which bears only the gloss of novelty without the rich depths of the authentic past is apt to appear hollow and immature. Peter DeVries delightfully caricatures such churchly bumptiousness in his description of the Reverend Andrew Mackerel's People's Liberal Church:

Our church is, I believe, the first split-level church in America. It has five rooms and two baths downstairs — dining area, kitchen and three parlors for committee and group meetings — with a crawl space behind the furnace ending in the hillside into which the structure is built. Upstairs is one huge all-purpose interior, divisible into different-sized components by means of sliding walls and convertible into an auditorium for putting on plays, a gymnasium for athletics and a ballroom for dances. There is a small worship area at one end. This has a platform cantilevered on both sides, with a free-form pulpit designed by Noguchi. It consists of a slab of marble set on four legs of four delicately differing fruitwoods, to symbolize the four Gospels, and their failure to harmonize. Behind it dangles a large multicolored mobile, its interdenominational parts swaying, as one might fancy, in perpetual reminder of the Pauline stricture against those "blown by every wind of doctrine." . . . Thus People's Church is a church designed to meet the needs of today, and to serve the whole man. [2]

People's Church in its architecture and its symbolism may speak to the modern mind but it does not say anything — at least nothing authentic about the Christian gospel. A symbol, in Calvin's terms, was to represent "things present" not "things absent." Our great need is for revitalized symbols representing the things of the gospel present to our congregations. If the liturgy and symbols of the church represent only the traditions of the past, they represent "things absent" in time and can at most evoke nostalgia and sentimentality. If the liturgy and symbols represent only contemporary interest, then the historical reality of the revelation of God in Christ is among the "things absent" and the effect is emptiness. If the language and thought concepts in which the sermon is cast are antiquarian, little meaning is conveyed through the words. Therefore, in preaching the Word, symbols must convey enduring truth in terms the contemporary mind can grasp and by which a man can relate to the theological ideas the preacher seeks to communicate. All symbols must partake of this quality of transcendence and immediacy, of ultimacy and concreteness. Cheap symbols distract, and obscure symbols conceal.

We do not invent a symbol by deciding that one is needed. That is why the serious student of worship will carefully evaluate the traditional and not be misled into the feeling that he can easily create worship practices that will convey reality. Neither will he be misled into the belief that anything antique is automatically authentic and therefore will communicate meaning. This is particularly true of visual symbols. Many of our visual symbols are obscure and even misleading. Horton Davies says, "I shall not quickly forget the delighted comment of my small son of seven when, looking at the carved symbols of the altar of the Episcopal Cathedral in San Francisco last summer, he pointed to the three interlinking circles, which for me, symbolized the Holy Trinity, but for him were immediately identifiable as 'Ballantine's Beer.'" Some visual aids no longer aid. In this area it may well be that more vivid representations in modern style will gradually be developed.

Symbols arise from the mind of an age as men grapple with reality and attempt to represent it. The art of architecture illustrates this fact. Slowly, laboriously, experimentally, buildings arise that in their design reflect the spirit of an age. In church architecture this has proved true. It may well be that we are on the verge of a genuine breakthrough in this area. For a long time, building committees were devoted to a false Gothic or a pseudocolonial on the grounds that " that is what a church ought to look like." We are now coming to see that a church of the twentieth century ought to symbolize our faith and our understanding of the nature of God, wedding the inner thrust of the gospel to the outer expression of our society, so vastly different from those societies that gave birth to Gothic and colonial design. The same thing is true of music. The great rebirth of congregational singing came when Luther infused authentic folk expressions with religious values. Yet Zwingli, though appreciating music greatly, forbade any use of it in the church. Calvin, a bit uncertain as to its influence, encouraged the use of the Psalter. When the organ was introduced, it was rejected as an instrument of worship by most Protestant churches and not until the latter half of the nineteenth century was it generally accepted. Opposition was especially strong among Presbyterians. Now what church among the main-line denominations would be without its organ, even though it be only an electronic substitute? By the beginning of the twentieth century, chancel areas were so arranged that a man from Mars might easily assume that organ pipes were objects of worship. Such are the changing practices and customs as each age gropes toward effective methods and symbols of praise.

It has been some time since any significant musical expression has arisen from within the church. The Gregorian chant has regained popularity in some circles, particularly Roman Catholic, but it is obviously not an authentic voice in which the twentieth century can give forth its praise. In line with the culture of the nineteenth century the frontier church created a folk music of sorts, and the great revivals gave birth to the gospel songs. It is equally obvious that the unsophisticated folk music can only be considered quaint by churchgoers today, and the gospel songs are the rock 'n' roll of sacred music, appealing only to the musical adolescent. The saccharine sentimentality of the music and the bad theology of many of the thoughts contained in the words make the gospel songs an inevitable casualty of time. There is still resistance to discarding them, but the resistance is based on associations that will weaken in another generation in most denominations. Their highly subjective and individualistic approach does not meet the needs of an age in which worship is again assuming more objectivity in a framework of social emphasis. Small circles of initiates have introduced the jazz motif in some experimental worship experiences. Jazz is expressive of our time with its note of loneliness and estrangement. It is authentic. However, it is doubtful that the musical symbols of worship will introduce the jazz theme on any widespread scale in our time. There is no theological reason against it, for there is no " sacred " music as such. There is only music which when it expresses something real and truly human can be used as a vehicle of religious experience. The Lutheran chorale embroidered secular themes, the Negro spiritual was a form of folk music, and most Protestant choir music derives from the opera in form. As in architecture, perhaps we stand on the verge of a major development in music for worship that will catch and hold the deep human needs of our age in lyrical expression of praise toward God. It remains to be seen whether we are spiritually capable of such an achievement.

In America, jazz or a modification of this musical form may be the medium of a new church music. It must come naturally, however, for symbols cannot be forced. Only as they express true aspirations in forms that speak to the hearts and for the hearts of worshipers can they be valid symbols. This is why we cannot simply move candles into the sanctuary, place collars and stoles upon our ministers and bronze crosses upon the Communion table, and decide that we are now making a creative use of symbols. Even when symbols out of the past have been introduced and liturgical formulas selected from the traditions of the church have been revived for regular use, we have only begun the task of revitalizing worship. We cannot escape the job of translating eternal truth into terms of the contemporary. For example, the liturgy of the church reflects little of the struggle for social justice both in the economic and the racial conflicts of our time. It reflects nothing of the great problem of war in the atomic age. Here arc points at which prayers and litanies may be made contemporary. Music and the hymns of the church may be a medium of voicing the aspirations of people toward brotherhood. Some of the better modern hymns fulfill this very need, but as yet they are unfamiliar to the majority of churchgoers. It might be that if John Oxenham's " In Christ There Is No East or West " had been as familiar to churchgoers in the South as " The Old Rugged Cross," a difference would have been shown in the response of the church to the racial crisis of recent years.

The worship of the church in the twentieth century must express continuity with the past and awareness of the present. G. Ernest Wright contrasts the worship of Israel with that of the polytheistic faiths of ancient times by saying: " In the faith of Israel the basis of worship lay in historical memory and in spiritual communion and obedience." [3] The Christian basis for faith lies in historical memory. The symbols that recreate this memory are indispensable. The basis of worship rests equally on spiritual communion and obedience. Symbols must not only recreate a memory, they must inspire to communion and obedience. The liturgy must bring the historical past into the present in such a way that response is required in terms of the im-

mediate. Thus far this book has dwelt primarily upon the
heritage, "the historical memory," of the church but let
there be no misunderstanding. The purpose of such an examination has been the conviction that "spiritual communion and obedience" may best be seen as we relate
ourselves to the past. Dr. Wright identifies the "most significant differentiation between Israelite and Christian religion on the one hand, and that of pagan religion on the
other" as a difference to be found at this very point.

In the worship of the Israelite and the Christian, primary attention is focused upon the great redeeming acts of God. In
worship these historical events are rehearsed and the worshiper
joins himself by sympathetic imagination with the original participants and understands that these acts were done for him
also (cf. Deut. 5:3; 26:3-1). He then gives thanks and praise to
God for what God has done, and solemnly renews his cove-
nanted vows. The spiritual process which biblical worship en-
tails thus involves a combination of historical narration with
participation by means of memory and imagination, with illumination derived from the continued working of God's spirit,
with praise and thanksgiving, and with solemn renewal of
covenant as the worshiper again faces his own life. Much more
than this is involved, depending upon the occasion and the
type of worship, yet illumination from historical memory and
participation remain central and primary. As such, the worship
avoids the pitfalls of magic and mysticism, but combines the
historical past, present, and future in the conception of God's
gracious and continuous direction of human life.[4]

The failure of much of the Protestantism of the seventeenth, eighteenth, and nineteenth centuries was a failure
at the point of rehearsal and involvement. For all its vaunted
Biblicism, or perhaps because of it, Protestantism was root-
less. The liturgical renewal of our time can succeed in its
purpose only if it draws upon the past and combines it with
present and future in creating through the experience of
worship a sense of the continuing acts of God's redemptive
purposes. This means a recognition, not in the sermon alone,
but in the liturgical acts of the congregation of such redemptive concerns as the great social issues of our age, the

ecumenical movement within the church, and the pressing problems of the Christian ethic in a world wherein that ethic has been increasingly rejected even as an ideal.

In what has been said can be found the essential answer to the criticism made by free-church advocates to the effect that an increased interest in liturgy is a form of escape from ethical concerns and social responsibility.

Bishop Robinson is right when he declares that " liturgy . . . can so easily simply create ' another world ' of its own, a world where everything is ' done ' according to the latest (or the oldest) models and which yet merely goes on side by side with real life." [5] For the word " liturgy " might be substituted the word " theology " or even the word " ethics." Dr. Ernest Trice Thompson has developed a graphic example of escape from the pressing claims of society upon the church as he has shown how the Presbyterian Church in the South fled to the refuge of a doctrine of " the spirituality of the church " in the slavery controversies of the antebellum period. This doctrine, which Thompson labels " a distinctive doctrine of the Presbyterian Church in the United States," grew stronger in the postwar period to the extent that it has dominated Southern Presbyterianism until very recent times.[6] Yet no Reformed tradition has been more influenced by the free-church worship of the nineteenth century than the Presbyterian Church in the United States. In many areas it remains as fiercely antiliturgical as its fellow Christians of Southern Baptist persuasion.

Perhaps worship may afford an escape from true involvement, but those who seek to evade the claims of life can and do find the means without fleeing to liturgical religion. Who would dare to say that the free churches have confronted the racial issue in our Southland more forthrightly than the liturgical churches? Have not many of the sect group and some major denominations concentrated on beer-drinking, dancing, card-playing, and Sabbath observance to avoid letting " justice roll down like waters, and righteousness like an everflowing stream "? Theology can be a haven from ethical sensitivity and has so proven itself. Evangelism can be a pious catchword to avoid involvement. There are innumerable roads of escape from commitment for those who desire to walk them. The liturgy is but one road and perhaps not the easiest.

Of course there are dangers in the liturgical renewal. Through the centuries the Russian Church, for example, has centered its genius upon a liturgical presentation of the faith to the neglect of theological and ethical concerns. It must be remembered, however, when we point to Russian Orthodoxy and decry it as an example of liturgical lethargy that the people to whom it has ministered have been largely illiterate and the political context within which it has ministered has been tyrannical Czarist or Communist. Perhaps Christianity would have disappeared completely from Russian life if it had not been for the rich rituals that have permeated every phase of everyday existence and are almost ineradicable, as the Soviet Government is finding out.

There are other dangers in an emphasis on the liturgical life of the church. Trivial and insignificant matters may become centers of controversy. The location of the pulpit, attention to minutiae of apparel, abnormal concern over punctiliousness of movement in conducting the service, can drain spiritual vitality. But is it not true that little minds will fasten on little things? The debilitating controversies over liturgical procedure are no more significant in Christian history than debilitating arguments over minutiae of theology, or of ecclesiastical orders, or even of details of behavior.

We live in an age that has been called post-Christian, post-Protestant, the age of secularism. The witness of the church to the eternal gospel is not a facile witness where it is effective and meaningful. The framework of society is not as markedly Christian in its outlines as we at least assume it once was. Christian assumptions are doubted; the Christian ethic is looked upon with cynicism or with nostalgia. The Christian story is only vaguely known. How best proclaim it?

Since beginning this manuscript I picked up Donald Soper's Beecher Lectures from my bedside table one night to read a few pages before going to sleep. In the chapter on " Evangelistic Preaching " by a man described in the jacket blurb as " one of the leading free churchmen of our day," widely known as a practitioner of open-air preaching, which he calls his " first love," I found an intriguing analysis of " stages of response which can be expected from preaching to the pagan, preaching to the porch, preaching to the pew, and preaching to the penitent form." Preaching to the pagans who are those of the " growing community which does not remember the Songs of Zion learnt at mother's knee, which cannot recite the Lord's prayer, and which has no nostalgia for religion whatsoever " involves the Christian witness of group work from which come volunteers for speaking in canteens and at street corners. The second group, who may be designated as those belonging to the porch, has memories of churchmanship, probably nostalgic, and are likely to be found in services on Easter and/or Christmas. This group needs the stimulation of renewed desire for churchgoing. Dr. Soper's insistence is that " the essence of the preaching in the porch is to evoke a response from those who are at present unprepared to take any radical part in churchmanship — to evoke a response from them at the point of liturgy, if it is impossible at this moment to expect a response at the point of decision in moral matters. . . . I believe that very largely the efficacy of their [the early Christians] preaching was contained in the participation evoked from the worshippers. Many of them, coming from Judaism, were not prepared to enter into a full understanding of the claims of the cross, but were drawn into the panoply, the beauty, and the activity of the church worship."

Dr. Soper's third group consists of those who are "hardened," or at least " regular," churchgoers. The evocation best expressed and demanded is a moral one — the moral imperative with a distinctly social emphasis. For the last group, those who offer the " penitent form," the setting must be " the tutelage of a whole pattern of Eucharistic worship. . . . What is decisive is that when those to whom we appeal have come at that point at which they can make a total response, then that total response should be made within the framework, the pattern, the ideology, the mysticism, the meaning, and all the imagery of the self-giving of Christ, the offering of Christ, the Totus Christus. . . . ' Do this, in remembrance of me.' . . . There is the heart and substance of true evangelical preaching." [7]

I have quoted these words and the ideas they express at some length because they come from the thought and experience of a man who has been an evangelist working out on the fringes of the church for years. They were delivered as part of the most noted lectureship on preaching in this country. What they emphasize and underline is that the medium of communication of the gospel today is worship, total worship that involves both spoken Word and Sacrament. This has been the essential thesis of this book. Without becoming sacerdotal, Protestantism needs to become sacramentarian. Without becoming liturgiologists in the formal and rigid sense, Protestants need to manifest a liturgy that will speak to modern man in his insecurities and frustrations. Without becoming symbolists, Protestants must use those valid symbols which speak to the whole person, which invade the subconscious as well as the conscious. Archbishop Temple in a famous definition of worship declares: " To worship is to quicken the conscience by the holiness of God, to feed the mind with the truth of God, to purge the imagination by the beauty of God, to open the heart to the love of God, to devote the will to the purpose of God."[8] Only in that experience of worship that draws on every resource can such a high aim be fulfilled.

If it is fulfilled to a more adequate degree in Protestantism, we may find ourselves closer than we had realized we were to our brethren of the Roman Catholic and the Orthodox churches. In an ecumenical age the difficulty of communicating doctrinally remains. Words are slippery, and doctrines must be interpreted in words. If we attempt to create an acceptable doctrine of the Lord's Supper, we shall probably entangle ourselves in verbal thickets. However, if we can gather around the Lord's Table we may create a fellowship in the atmosphere of a common symbol that will enable us to worship together and in our worship realize a oneness deeper than intellectual agreement. This is not said in order to brush aside the tremendous complications of theological dialogue. Such dialogue must go on, but the possibility of reaching consensus on doctrine is remote at the present time. The possibility of common worship is not nearly so remote as it seemed ten years ago. There are some emerging points of agreement — for one, the centrality of the Eucharist and for another, the need for active participation in the liturgy. As the Roman Catholic churches move toward invigorated preaching, congregational singing, and emphasis upon the public corporate celebration of the Mass, Protestant churches are moving toward deepened appreciation of Communion, congregational activity in the service as a whole, and a developing sense of the corporate life of the congregation within the church universal. Behind these changes lie theological and Biblical values that give them sturdy foundations. Perhaps our age is on the verge of discovering new places of worship whereunto the hurt and the hopeful, the frustrated and the fearless, the sinner and the saint, may repair.

Notes

Notes

PREFACE

1. Quoted by Luccock and Brentano, *The Questing Spirit* (Coward-McCann, Inc., 1947), p. 640.

CHAPTER 1.   INTRODUCTION

1. Herbert Wallace Schneider, *Religion in 20th Century America* (Harvard University Press, 1952), p. 149.

2. The word is used in its ordinary, everyday sense, not in the technical psychological sense. No attempt is made to attribute to human nature a special " impulse " to worship. Instead, there would seem to be a universal inclination on the part of human beings to respond to the world around and to relate to a world beyond the senses. This is the essence of worship.

3. Robert McAfee Brown, *The Spirit of Protestantism* (Oxford University Press, 1961), p. 132.

4. William Temple, *The Hope of a New World* (The Macmillan Company, 1943), p. 26.

5. Ilion T. Jones, *A Historical Approach to Evangelical Worship* (Abingdon Press, 1954), p. 216.

6. See H. Wheeler Robinson on " The Psychology of Language " in *Redemption and Revelation* (Harper & Brothers, 1942), pp. 39 ff.

7. Donald M. Baillie, *The Theology of the Sacraments: And Other Papers* (Charles Scribner's Sons, 1957), p. 51.

8. Jones, *op. cit.*, p. 217.

9. Alexander Miller, *The Man in the Mirror* (Doubleday & Company, Inc., 1958), p. 144.

10. Hugh Thomson Kerr, Jr., ed., *A Compend of Luther's Theology* (The Westminster Press, 1943), p. 142.

CHAPTER 2. TEMPLE, SYNAGOGUE, AND UPPER ROOM

1. Jones, *op. cit.*, p. 35.

2. C. F. D. Moule, *Worship in the New Testament* (John Knox Press, 1961), pp. 9–10.

3. For varying views, see Dom Gregory Dix, *The Shape of the Liturgy* (London: The Dacre Press, 1945); Max Thurian, *The Eucharistic Memorial*, Part II, *The New Testament* (John Knox Press, 1961, paperback); Oscar Cullmann and F. J. Leenhardt, *Essays on the Lord's Supper*, tr. by J. G. Davies (John Knox Press, 1958, paperback); C. F. D. Moule, *Worship in the New Testament* (John Knox Press, 1962, paperback). Dix's is the most exhaustive work on the whole subject of the liturgy of the Eucharist. It is not to be followed blindly and without reference to other works in this area. The last-named books are relatively brief but careful monographs that present the most recent research on the subject of origins.

4. Rudolf Bultmann, *Theology of the New Testament*, Vol. 1 (Charles Scribner's Sons, 1951), p. 58.

5. Cullmann and Leenhardt, *op. cit.*, p. 7.

6. *Ibid.*, pp. 17–19.

CHAPTER 3. THE WORD AND THE TABLE

1. Ray C. Petry, ed., *A History of Christianity: Readings in the History of the Early and Medieval Church* (Prentice-Hall, Inc., 1962), pp. 13–14.

2. *Ibid.*, p. 22.

3. Hans Lietzmann, *The Founding of the Church Universal* (Charles Scribner's Sons, 1938), pp. 165–166.

4. See Petry, *op. cit.*; Lietzmann, *op. cit.*; Henry Bettenson, ed., *Documents of the Christian Church* (Oxford University Press, 1947).

5. William D. Maxwell, *An Outline of Christian Worship: Its Development and Forms* (London: Oxford University Press, 1936), p. 16.

6. T. S. Garrett, *Christian Worship: An Introductory Outline* (London: Oxford University Press, 1961), p. 68.

7. George Hedley, *Christian Worship: Some Meanings and Means* (The Macmillan Company, 1953), pp. 187–188.

CHAPTER 4. THE WORD LOST IN SYMBOLS

1. Maxwell, *op. cit.*, p. 45.

2. Dix, *op. cit.*, p. 459.

3. Maxwell, *op. cit.*, p. 56.

4. Oscar Hardman, *A History of Christian Worship*

(Cokesbury Press, 1938), p. 57.

5. Dix, *op. cit.*, p. 36.

6. George E. McCracken and Allen Cabaniss, eds., *Early Medieval Theology*, The Library of Christian Classics, Vol. IX (The Westminster Press, 1957), p. 91.

7. See Bettenson, ed., *op. cit.*, p. 210.

CHAPTER 5.   THE TABLE BECOMES THE ALTAR

1. Maxwell, *op. cit.*, p. 65.

2. Will Durant, *The Age of Faith* (Simon and Schuster, Inc., 1950), p. 893.

3. *Ibid.*, p. 894.

4. Donald M. Baillie, *op. cit.*, p. 96.

5. Yngve Brilioth, *Eucharistic Faith and Practice: Evangelical and Catholic* (London: S.P.C.K., 1956), p. 89.

6. Hardman, *op. cit.*, p. 128.

7. *Ibid.*, p. 129.

8. *Ibid.*, p. 126.

9. Edwin Charles Dargan, *A History of Preaching*, Vol. 1 (Baker Book House, 1954), p. 230.

10. *Ibid.*, p. 300.

CHAPTER 6.   THE WORD AND THE REFORMATION

1. Maxwell, *op. cit.*, pp. 69–71.

2. *Ibid.*, pp. 79–80.

3. Kerr, *op. cit.*, p. 170.

4. *Ibid.*, p. 171.

5. *Ibid.*

6. Roland Bainton, *Here I Stand: A Life of Martin Luther* (Mentor Book, The New American Library, 1950), p. 250.

CHAPTER 7.   THE WORD AMONG THE CALVINISTS

1. Maxwell, *op. cit.*, pp. 72–73.

2. Jones, *op. cit.*, p. 125.

3. Bard Thompson, *Liturgies of the Western Church* (The World Publishing Company, 1961), p. 160.

4. *Ibid.*, pp. 162–163.

5. Quoted by Maxwell, *op. cit.*, pp. 100–101.

6. *Ibid.*, p. 111.

7. *Ibid.*, p. 115.

8. Thompson, *op. cit.*, p. 189.

9. Based on complete text in Thompson, *op. cit.*, pp. 197 ff.

10. C. J. Cadoux on " Zwingli " in *Christian Worship*, edited

by Nathaniel Micklem (London: Oxford University Press, 1936), p. 148.

11. Baillie, *op. cit.*, pp. 99–100.

12. Hugh T. Kerr, ed., *A Compend of the Institutes of the Christian Religion by John Calvin* (The Westminster Press, 1964, paperback), pp. 177–178.

CHAPTER 8.   THE WORD AMONG THE SCOTS AND THE ENGLISH

1. Garrett, *op. cit.*, p. 134.

2. Dix, *op. cit.*, p. 659.

3. Thompson, *op. cit.*, p. 289.

4. William Craft Dickinson, *John Knox's History of the Reformation in Scotland*, Vol. 2 (Philosophical Library, Inc., 1950), p. 313.

5. Based on Charles W. Baird, *The Presbyterian Liturgies* (Baker Book House, 1960), pp. 119 ff.

6. Will Durant, *The Reformation* (Simon and Schuster, Inc., 1957), p. 619.

7. Will and Ariel Durant, *The Age of Reason Begins* (Simon and Schuster, Inc., 1961), p. 205.

8. *Ibid.*, pp. 190–191.

9. Baird, *op. cit.*, p. 153.

10. Durant, *The Age of Reason Begins*, p. 192.

11. Jones, *op. cit.*, pp. 136–137.

CHAPTER 9.   THE WORD AMONG THE PURITANS

1. S. Arthur Devan, *Ascent to Zion* (The Macmillan Company, 1942), p. 70.

2. *Ibid.*, p. 73.

3. Maxwell, *op. cit.*, p. 132.

4. Howard G. Hageman, *Pulpit and Table* (John Knox Press, 1962), p. 43.

5. Evelyn Underhill, *Worship* (Harper & Brothers, 1936), p. 294.

6. Quoted by Maxwell, *op. cit.*, p. 134.

7. Hageman, *op. cit.*, pp. 47, 58, 59.

8. Kenneth Scott Latourette, *Advance Through Storm* (Harper & Brothers, 1945), p. 444.

9. Horton Davies, *Worship and Theology in England: From Watts and Wesley to Maurice, 1690–1850* (Princeton University Press, 1961), pp. 70, 75.

10. George M. Stephenson, *The Puritan Heritage* (The Macmillan Company, 1952), p. 31.

CHAPTER 10.   THE WORD ON THE AMERICAN FRONTIER

1. William Warren Sweet, *Religion in the Development of American Culture, 1765–1840* (Charles Scribner's Sons, 1952), p. 8.

2. Leonard J. Trinterud, *The Forming of an American Tradition: A Re-examination of Colonial Presbyterianism* (The Westminster Press, 1949), p. 241.

3. *Ibid.*, p. 304.

4. Quoted by Sidney E. Mead, " The Rise of the Evangelical Conception of the Ministry in America: 1607–1850," in *The Ministry in Historical Perspectives*, edited by H. Richard Niebuhr and Daniel D. Williams (Harper & Brothers, 1956), p. 239.

5. *Ibid.*, pp. 239–240.

6. Sweet, *op. cit.*, pp. 152–153.

7. *Ibid.*, pp. 156–157.

8. *Ibid.*, p. 157.

9. *Ibid.*, p. 158.

10. *Ibid.*, p. 159.

11. Jerald C. Brauer, *Protestantism in America: A Narrative History* (The Westminster Press, 1953), p. 114.

12. *Ibid.*, p. 116.

CHAPTER 11.   THE BEGINNINGS OF LITURGICAL RENEWAL

1. Jones, *op. cit.*, pp. 155–156.

2. J. Edgar Park, *The Miracle of Preaching* (The Macmillan Company, 1936), p. 113.

3. William D. Maxwell, *A History of Worship in the Church of Scotland* (London, Oxford University Press, 1955), p. 175.

4. Hageman, *op. cit.*, p. 67.

5. See Hageman, *op. cit.*, pp. 84 ff.

6. For a full account of this movement, see James Hastings Nichols, *Romanticism in American Theology* (The University of Chicago Press, 1961).

7. Baird, *op. cit.*, pp. 254–255.

8. *Ibid.*, pp. 262–265.

9. Massey Hamilton Shepherd, Jr., *The Eucharist and Liturgical Renewal* (Oxford University Press, 1960), p. 89.

10. Davies, *op. cit.*, pp. 280–282.

11. Ernest R. Sandeen, " Worship and Ecclesiology in American History," *The Pulpit*, June, 1963, p. 23.

12. Mary G. Powell, *The History of Old Alexandria, Virginia* (The William Byrd Press, 1928), p. 104.

CHAPTER 12. THE FORCES IN LITURGICAL RENEWAL

1. Pehr Edwall, Eric Hayman, William D. Maxwell, eds., *Ways of Worship: The Report of a Theological Commission of Faith and Order* (Harper & Brothers, 1951), p. 20.

2. Arthur Carl Piepkorn, "The Protestant Worship Revival and the Lutheran Liturgical Movement," in *The Liturgical Renewal of the Church*, edited by Massey Hamilton Shepherd, Jr. (Oxford University Press, 1960), pp. 66–67.

3. Willard L. Sperry, *Reality in Worship* (The Macmillan Company, 1932), p. 278.

4. *Ibid.*, pp. 278–279.

5. *Ibid.*, p. 277.

6. *Ibid.*, pp. 282 ff.

7. Von Ogden Vogt, *Modern Worship* (Yale University Press, 1927), p. 53.

8. Albert W. Palmer, *The Art of Conducting Public Worship* (The Macmillan Company, 1942), p. 25.

9. Hageman, *op. cit.*, p. 99.

10. James Bissett Pratt, *The Religious Consciousness* (The Macmillan Company, 1940), p. 307.

11. James Bissett Pratt, *Eternal Values in Religion* (The Macmillan Company, 1950), p. 151.

CHAPTER 13. PRESENT EMPHASES IN LITURGICAL RENEWAL

1. John H. S. Kent, "Worship and Theology," *The Expository Times*, October, 1962, p. 11.

2. Cullmann and Leenhardt, *op. cit.*, p. 16.

3. Dix, *op. cit.*, p. 12.

4. Baillie, *op. cit.*, p. 44.

5. A. J. Gossip, *The Galilean Accent* (Edinburgh: T. & T. Clark, 1926), p. 260.

6. See *Service for the Lord's Day and Lectionary for the Christian Year* (The Westminster Press, 1964).

7. Edwall, Hayman, Maxwell, *op. cit.*, p. 30.

8. Hageman, *op. cit.*, p. 121.

CHAPTER 14. THE WORD IN TRADITION AND IN SYMBOLS

1. *Presbyterian Outlook*, March 16, 1964, p. 13.

2. Charles W. F. Smith, *Biblical Authority for Modern Preaching* (The Westminster Press, 1960), p. 57.

3. William D. Maxwell, *A History of Worship in the Church of Scotland* (London: Oxford University Press, 1955), p. 133.

4. *Ibid.*, p. 175.

5. Amos N. Wilder, *Theology and Modern Literature* (Harvard University Press, 1958), p. 50.

CHAPTER 15. RENEWAL THROUGH WORSHIP

1. G. A. Studdert-Kennedy, *I Believe* (George H. Doran Company, n.d.), p. 22.

2. Peter DeVries, *The Mackerel Plaza* (Signet Books, The New American Library, 1959), p. 10.

3. G. Ernest Wright, "The Faith of Israel," *The Interpreter's Bible*, Vol. I (Abingdon-Cokesbury Press, 1952), p. 375.

4. *Ibid.*, pp. 377–378.

5. John A. T. Robinson, *Honest to God* (The Westminster Press, 1963), pp. 89–90.

6. Ernest Trice Thompson, *The Spirituality of the Church* (John Knox Press, 1961).

7. Donald Soper, *The Advocacy of the Gospel* (London: Hodder & Stoughton, Ltd., 1961), pp. 88–100.

8. Temple, *op. cit.*, p. 30.

Index